CACTUS PRYOR
Inside Texas

PARADE MARSHALS

CACTUS PRYOR
Inside Texas

Commentaries from KLBJ-AM, Austin, Texas

SHOAL CREEK PUBLISHERS, INC.

Bryan, Texas 77801

Published by Shoal Creek Publishers, Inc.
Copyright © 1982 by Richard Pryor
Special thanks to the management of KLBJ-AM, Austin, Texas

ACKNOWLEDGEMENTS

For this book I am indebted to veteran publisher Luther Thompson who invited . . . writer Sherry Benn who encouraged . . . KLBJ radio general manager Ted Smith who ramrodded . . . Beth Belkonen who corrected, corrected, corrected . . . Walter Cronkite who "out fore-worded himself" . . . and to Jewell Pryor who shared.

Library of Congress Cataloging in Publication Data

Pryor, Richard
Cactus Pryor Inside Texas

LC 82-062069
ISBN 0-88319-063-X (sc)
0-88319-062-1 (hc)

Manufactured in the United States of America
THIRD PRINTING

I dedicate this book to the "friends and neighbors out there in radio land" who listened . . . and to Lady Bird Johnson, who provided the microphone without question.

Foreword

Cactus Pryor is not a self-satisfied man. At least not in the sense that he displays an overbearing smugness offensive to his less talented fellow men. But if he isn't secretly pleased with himself, then he's a darned fool—and that, all who have been privileged to know him agree, he is not.

Cactus made his choice a long time ago and he has stuck with it despite blandishments of fame and fortune that would have tempted most of us. His choice was to be a big fish (very, very big) in a small pond (not so small, at that) rather than the big fish he would still have been in a much larger pond. Despite great successes before audiences around the nation and a lot of lucrative offers to headquarter elsewhere, Cactus stayed home.

He has thus given his native Austin a rare gift that few cities anywhere can claim—a real live humorist with the sharp eye, the quick tongue, the educated pen, and, most important, the warm heart to record in sometimes hilarious detail its fashions and foibles.

He, of course, has had a rich vein to mine. Texas *is* bigger than life, and what Cactus has done here is prove that many of those who populate the state today are no less characters than the old-timers who contributed to the rich lore of the Lone Star State.

Cactus wears on his sleeve his fondness for a disappearing Texas, but his bemusement at the Texas that is replacing it is not marked by bitterness.

And maybe that's because the old Texas is not *really* disappearing. Maybe what Cactus is telling us here is that while a lot of his precious Texas hill country is being bulldozed and paved, there is no way to bury beneath mass-produced modernity the irrepressible uniqueness of Texas or Texans.

Cactus himself is one of a kind—a masterful story-teller in the tradition of Texas' best, and this collection of his radio essays is a testament to that.

WALTER CRONKITE

I have been in radio since 1944. All but two of those years were spent at Lady Bird Johnson's radio station in Austin—KTBC, later changed to KLBJ. For a number of years I have delivered a daily commentary on whatever views I chose to share with my audience. More often than not, the subject matter was Texas. I am an incurable Texan—chauvinistic, proud, and frequently blind. If there is anything worse than a proud Texan, it's a proud Austin, Texan. I have had a life-long love affair with this capital city that my forebears had the good sense to locate in over one hundred years ago. And I have shared this affection with my radio audience on numerous occasions.

I write for the ear, usually hastily on paper napkins, backs of bills, and frequently on airsickness bags aboard a Braniff or Texas International flight from one Texas city to another. A daily deadline when added to dozens of others dictates some strange writing desks. There's a certain frustration when writing for radio. Once your words have gone into the air, they very seldom return, and you wonder where they went, if anywhere. So I welcome this opportunity to share these ear words with your eyes. I welcome this opportunity to share my Texas with Texans from any state or country. These words are delivered with dedicated bias and, I think without exception, with love.

CACTUS PRYOR

Me and Richard Pryor

I'm frequently asked why I'm called "Cactus." I'm frequently *not* asked that question, too. Because a lot of people, like Rhett, frankly don't give a damn. I've got a stock answer for those who do question. Because, I say, my real name is Richard Pryor. But the brilliant Black comedian has pretty well cornered that name in show business circles, and although I was Richard Pryor long before he was, it behooves me to go by "Cactus."

Actually, I was tagged a cacti because my father owned the Cactus Theatre in Austin. Every time I stood before an audience, I would add a commercial for Dad's movies. He got the plug and I got stuck with the name. I've been a Cactus for some time.

At times, however, I resort to the legal "Richard." The Internal Revenue Service, Social Security, the United States Air Force, and my wife when mad, know me as Richard Pryor.

I once did a one-nighter convention show in Las Vegas at one of the plush hotels on the strip. When I go to that treacherous city I make it a point to reconfirm my plane reservations home. That way I know I will at least get back with me, if nothing else. I called the airline reservation agent, giving my name as "R. Pryor."

"Yes sir, Mr. Pryor. We have your reservation confirmed. Uh, does that 'R' by any chance stand for Richard?"

"Yes, it does," I admitted.

"Well, what a pleasure it is to talk to you, Mr. Pryor. I'm quite a fan of yours."

"Well, thank you very much," I gladly responded.

"I didn't know you were in town, Mr. Pryor. Where are you playing?"

"Oh, I did a show at the Tropicana last night," I truthfully replied.

"Well, I'm sure they loved it. Uh, Mr. Pryor, I notice that you're flying coach. I'm sure the reservation agent made a mistake. Might we upgrade you to first class, as our guest, of course?"

"Why, of course," I merrily agreed. "That would be very nice of you."

"Might we send a limousine for you? It would be our pleasure."

"And mine too," I concurred.

"Good. Your driver will be at the Tropicana at eight in the morning."

The next morning in front of the hotel there was a black limousine that would have done any funeral proud. I went up to the properly liveried chauffeur and asked, "Is this the limousine for Richard Pryor?"

"Yes it is, sir."

"Well, I'm Richard Pryor."

"I'm waiting for Richard Pryor the comedian, sir."

"I'm Richard Pryor the comedian."

"I'm waiting for Richard Pryor the comedian who played here at the Tropicana last night, sir."

"I am the Richard Pryor who played here at the Tropicana last night." I presented my billfold with proper identification. The chauffeur looked me over with jaundiced eye and said simply, "You've been sick, ain't you?"

I'll never be taken to any airport in better style, and I got my first-class seat, too. Richard, anytime you want to be a Cactus I owe you one.

Star Trek

Anytime I received a call from Conrad Brady with Interstate Theatres in Dallas, I knew that I was going to be chopping in tall cotton for awhile. Conrad was in charge of the personal appearances of the various movie stars in the Interstate Theatre Circuit that covered the state of Texas. When the stars were signed to long-term contracts with the movie studios, they were often required to come out into the real world and make stage appearances in connection with their movies. It was my happy task to emcee those appearances for Interstate Theatres. That meant for a week or so I would be touring with the stars and sampling a lifestyle of limousines, gourmet foods, luxurious hotel suites, and adoring throngs of movie fans that was as foreign to me as doing a love scene with Marilyn Monroe. It also meant the opportunity to view the likes of John Wayne, James Stewart, Charlton Heston, Fred MacMurray, Chill Wills, Dean Martin, Audie Murphy, Raquel Welch, and Katharine Ross close up.

With all modesty, most of these stars badly needed me. They were usually lost on stage without written lines to deliver. So it fell upon me to bring them out and make them seem like real people to the theater audiences. This sometimes presented a physical problem. With Chuck Connors and Clint Walker, I had to stand my five feet nine on the top of a Coke box in order to reach the microphone we were sharing. Audie Murphy presented another problem. He was our most courageous and decorated soldier in World War II, but he was a craven coward when it came to a live audience. Bringing him out before an audience was a harder job than getting me on the firing line. Not so Chill Wills—the problem was getting him off the stage. Dean Martin, I was told, would not appear on stage—only stand

Onstage with Sandra Dee, Jimmy Stewart.

in the audience when introduced. I tempted him with the microphone, and we did thirty minutes together.

Raquel Welch was the toughest to deal with. It was enough to ruin your fantasies. Backstage she was demanding and temperamental, but on-stage she couldn't have been more charming. Once on a tour with Jimmy Stewart she stood up the press at a scheduled conference. Mild-mannered Stewart towered over the surprisingly short Welch, placed his long arm around her shoulder, and said, in essence, "If you do that again, honey, I'm going to change your exciting dimensions." She became Mary Poppins. Stewart was a dream to work with—devoid of temperament, eager to please, and willing to work from dawn to midnight even in a July west Texas sun.

John Wayne seemed to enjoy the contact with his fans more than any of the stars. He'd wade right into the middle of a mob of them, slapping backs, pumping hands, kissing babies of all ages. He could have been LBJ playing a crowd. I was amazed at the number of women, many of them very young, who offered their company to him. His standard reply was, "Where were you when I needed you?"

Except for a gruelling schedule, the stars were pampered like royalty on these tours. There was a very nervous young man from the studio to tend to their every wish. There were clusters of them to laugh even at remarks that *may* have been meant to be humorous. The ladies came complete with hairdressers. Some of the male stars came complete with hair rufflers—groupies of the fifties and sixties.

Always these tours would end at the house of Big John Hamilton in San Antonio. Flamboyant Hamilton was well-known by most of the stars—he even appeared in a number of John Wayne's movies. But his parties for the visiting stars were more popular with the Hollywood set than were the infamous Hollywood parties. It was the first time I saw a one-hundred-yard backstroke race swum in pure Cutty Sark.

Then, at the end of the week, the stars would go back

to their movie sets and mansions and I would head back to my five a.m. disc jockey show wondering why all of the sudden I felt so let down, even though still slightly exhilarated, by the memory of the movie fan who had asked me for my autograph, thinking I was Katharine Ross's father.

Vietnam in Georgia

The threatening crack of small arms fire greeted me as I arrived in the Vietnamese village. On the horizon, American planes were dropping napalm bombs, the flames racing across the scarred land like volcanoes erupting horizontally. The tallest structure in the village was one-half of a church. The other half had obviously been destroyed by shell fire. The entire area was surrounded by barbed wire and ditches filled with pungi sticks, bamboo poles sharpened to a razor's edge and dipped in human excrement. Vietnamese natives were running for shelter. Green Beret troops were manning barricades, their weapons ready.

Just outside the defense perimeter a bright red flare had been set off, its smoke defining the direction of the wind. A giant American helicopter roared over the tops of the jungle trees and quickly lowered itself to the ground adjacent to the flare. The doors opened and a huge man wearing the familiar green beret and a camouflaged uniform jumped out, followed by a small group of similarly dressed soldiers. As they drew closer, I noticed that the man in the lead was John Wayne.

I was there on the set of the movie "The Green Berets" because I had tested John Wayne. A few months before, I had emceed a dinner in honor of his sixtieth birthday at Six Flags Inn in Arlington. I wanted to see if the guy could take it as well as he gave it. So I twisted his tail pretty severely with barbed humor. He loved it. I suspect Cutty Sark was as much a factor in his enjoyment as was my humor. Several weeks later I received a call from Wayne asking me if I would accept a role in the film he was making at Fort Benning, Georgia. For this military assignment I gladly volunteered.

It was a rare opportunity to watch the legend at work.

An appreciative audience—John Wayne (center), Jack Valenti (next to Cactus).

The movie was John Wayne's philosophical statement regarding the Vietnamese war. He was pure hawk and this was his rebuttal to the doves. He had visited Vietnam, had heard the whine of bullets, and he really wanted to be there fighting. Instead, he brought the war to Georgia. He starred as the commanding officer of the Green Beret Company. He also was the director of the film. But as the days went along he kept confusing the two jobs. The director became more and more the C.O. I was glad that I was on his side and not one of the Orientals playing the role of the Vietcong. During the combat scenes his eyes would narrow to that ominous squint and you knew that Colonel John Wayne was really in Vietnam, taking on the Cong.

His young son, Ethan, inherited his father's dislike of the commies. One day at lunch the boy was seated across the table from George Takei of "Star Trek" fame, who was dressed in the uniform of a Vietcong captain. He picked up an apple and hit the "damned commie" right between his Oriental eyes. Father Wayne backhanded his son halfway down the table, then swept him up in a bear hug and explained to the boy that George was actually a Democrat, which is not quite as bad as a commie.

Like all wars, this one dragged on too long. The Georgia trees that played the role of the Vietnamese jungle began to turn autumn gold, so the studio called in reinforcements to give director Wayne some relief, and the movie had to be finished in more tropical Florida. The cost overrun, the time overrun, the critics' reviews all confirmed the fact that war is indeed hell. Rack up another victory for the Vietcong.

"Coming out of chute number five," the pretty contestants for queen of the Stonewall Peach Festival.

The Stonewall Peach Festival

"Now friends and neighbors, take a deep seat and get a faraway look in your eyes. They're coming out of chute number five."

No, it wasn't the rodeo announcer at the annual Stonewall, Texas, Peach Festival announcing the bucking bronc event. It was me as emcee of the Stonewall Peach Festival Queen Contest introducing the contestants for the peach queen of Gillespie county. And the lovely little ladies literally did make their entrance into the rodeo arena where the pageant was being presented through the same chute that the bucking horses and wild Brahma bulls made theirs.

For twenty years I have emceed this beauty pageant. And each year my fee is the same—all the Stonewall peaches I can carry home and a box seat over the rodeo pens for my family and me to watch the rodeo. Not for me the chili cookoffs, the armadillo festivals, the Willie Nelson picnics. I like my country fairs pure, where the cowboy boots are properly broken in with cow manure and the Stetsons are meant to ward off sun and rain, not attract attention.

The Stonewall Peach Festival is the real thing. It's a celebration of life in the Texas hill country, of the harvest, of the indescribably delicious peaches, of the reward of hard work and the sheer fun of rodeoing, of cold-beer drinking, of washer pitching, of barbecue eating, and of pretty-gal watching. There is a practical aspect to the festival, too. The afternoon peach auction brings in big money; astronomical sums are paid for the pick of the crop in various categories.

The spectators are mostly hill country folks of Germanic stock. You hear more German guttural than Texas twang. However, some of the world's dignitaries have enjoyed the festival fun as guests of the Lyndon Johnsons, who, natives will tell you, "ranch just across the river yonder." I'll never forget the conversation between world-famous hostess Perle Mesta and LBJ's cousin Oriole at one of these festivals.

"What do yo do, Miz Mesta?"

"Why, I give parties."

"Give parties! Now what kind of a do is that?"

The Johnson family's guests enjoy the fruits of the farmers' labors year 'round. The ranchhouse cooks are the world's best at preparing Stonewall peach desserts.

In the early days, the queen contest was held during half-time of the rodeo. The queen was seated on her throne in the middle of the arena on an island of funeral parlor grass. The contestants had to walk about fifty yards in high heels and flowing homemade gowns over spongy, sandy loam. It was the only beauty contest in America where the girl's poise was determined by the manner in which she circumnavigated piles of residue deposited by the preceding animal performers. Adding to their dilemma was the current hair fashion of that time, upswept bouffants, spray-netted until you could have used them as a tennis backboard. The usual Texas wind blowing off these sail-like surfaces would test a girl's strength as well as her poise. The curtsies to the queen were scarier than the bull rides. You never knew if the contestant was going to make it up on her feet again.

The question-and-answer sessions were not exactly Atlantic City. The girls may not have known which President said "The only thing to fear is fear itself," but they could give you more important knowledge—their personal recipe for peach pie or cobbler and how many bushels you could expect from a healthy peach tree.

The peach queen contest became more sophisticated over the years. A flatbed truck was added to serve as a stage. And finally, a real stage was constructed over the stock pens so that the beauties now rise above the beasts below. And a contestant can walk without having to watch what she might be stepping in—just like Miss America.

Willie Nelson in Vegas

I was a coal in Newcastle—an Austinite who went to see Willie Nelson in Las Vegas. I'll go see Willie anywhere, anytime. But I especially wanted to see him in the ultra plush showroom of Caesar's Palace. I was curious to see what sort of treatment Vegas gave the outlaw, what they might try to do with him. After all, the city is the mecca of show biz glitter. It's tinsel town augmented with neon. It's rhinestone and furs, not blue jeans and tennis shoes.

The dazzling signs outside the casinos are outdone only by the costumes worn by the performers inside. Every move on stage is carefully orchestrated and designed for audience effect. So I was anxious to see how they handled laid-back Willie. I soon learned the answer. They don't. Willie handles Las Vegas just like he handles Luckenbach or the old Armadillo World Headquarters or the Texas Opry House.

It was beautiful. The showroom was full of a Heinz mixture of Mafia rich, west and east coast highbrow, Amarillo lowbrow, and surgical-stocking, package-tour tourists. They were there in red polyester and blue fox—sometimes on the same person. Naturally, there were a lot of Texas urban and rural cowboys and cowgirls on hand too.

There was no showline of chorus girls to bring the act on. The band just strolled onto a dimly lit stage. While tuning their instruments, they drank their beer and smoked their cigarettes—just like at home. Then a guy wearing a black hat bigger than the rest of his body crawled onto a stool; the spotlights came on. He sang a song about Willie, another about Lubbock, told a couple of dope jokes, and left. I suppose he was the warm-up act, but Willie didn't follow like the main act is supposed to do after the warm-up. The band had another Lone Star. They talked among themselves on the still dimly lit stage, and a figure walked out carrying a guitar. He engaged in conversation with the band. When he turned to the audience, a spotlight bathed him, and Willie Nelson broke out into a chorus of "Whiskey River." Simultaneously, a huge Texas flag dropped like the shade on a moonshiner's window to form the backdrop for his performance. The crowd went wild and stayed that way through an unusually long (for Las Vegas) two-hour performance.

Willie and the band dressed in their usual Texas style for their show at swank Caesar's Palace. Willie wore a black sleeveless tee shirt, blue jeans, boots, and, of course, the red bandana around his head. No special, cutesy, inside-Vegas material. Just *pure dee pure* Willie Nelson music with only a "thank you" in between numbers. We could have been in a Texas honky-tonk except for the excellent lighting to focus attention on the soloists.

Frequently there were shouts of "We love you, Willie!" from the audience. One overly liquified cowboy strived vainly time after time to make his way to the stage so that he might touch his god, only to be reseated by the attendants. He was drawn by the magnet playing the battered guitar and singing the songs. I've never heard Willie or the band sound better. They were obviously having fun. So was the audience, all one thousand of us . . . at thirty-four dollars a head.

Yes sir, the Texas traildrivers came to town on a Saturday night and took over the town. The town had nothing to do but enjoy it.

The Fund Raiser

I attended a traditional American ritual the other night in another city—the political testimonial dinner. A gathering of all the faithful at one hundred dollars per plate to bear witness to their chosen messiah, who will lead his constituents from the wilderness to the promised land of lower taxes, more services, and more milk and honey. I enjoy these orgies of adulation despite the clichés, the exaggerations, the hypocrisy, the cold food, and the long hours, because if you are a people-watcher—especially a political people-watcher—they are the ultimate in American political melodrama.

The script is always the same, the cast and the scene. The colors are always red, white, and blue. The location is always the convention center or the high school gymnasium. Always the play opens with the star and his wife standing bravely at the door to welcome all those who have come to pay tribute, a hundred-dollar tribute. He not content to pump hands but also slapping special backs or kissing special cheeks. She smiling valiantly despite aching feet, desperately searching her mind to relate names to faces. And the visiting politicians perusing the crowd like sea gulls looking for cut bait and, when spotting a live one, swooping down, offering no chance for escape. And always, the arm around the shoulder, the mouth to the ear, the old practiced pitch.

Usually there's a fiddle band from the district to make with the background music, and if you're lucky the amplifiers are turned down enough to allow conversation. If they're not, the conversation goes on anyway, though mostly unheard.

Before the meal, the invocation is given, probably by the supporting Catholic priest, saving the Baptist preacher for the benediction. Both imply that if God had a vote it would certainly go to the man being honored. Then we toastmasters make with our clichés, the ribs, the roasts, the introduction of the disciples at the headtable, the important recognition of the other political figures scattered throughout the audience, the credits for decorations, food, ticket sales, childbearing, arm twisting, and the inevitable telegrams of regret and congratulation. And before the messiah, testimony from other messiahs, the visiting politicos who declare with all apparent sincerity that the future of the country depends upon the support of the one being honored.

And finally, late into the night, the anointed one speaks and speaks and speaks. "Too many to single any one person out," the script goes, but before he is through none have missed being recognized. Then comes the admission that it is all possible because of the devotion and dedication of the loyal spouse—she blushes appropriately—and the love and guidance of the wonderful parents—they beam sufficiently. Then come the promises, followed by the final appeal to the great politician in the sky.

The evening ends with the final flurry of handpumping and backslapping around the headtable. Another American phenomenon concluded, and the most phenomenal fact about the whole show is that it's part of a system that works.

The Sharpstown Scandal

Sharpstown hit Texas like a blue norther in July. It was a shocker. Texas politicians were falling like Lone Star beer caps at the New Braunfels Wurstfest. Austin was so nervous it registered on the Richter scale.

Many of the names being mentioned in connection with the stock scandal were household names throughout the state. Many, though innocent, were assumed guilty by timing—they had simply picked the wrong time to be in office. Men like Lieutenant Governor Ben Barnes and Governor Preston Smith (though never indicted) would never recover from the fallout of the bomb that landed squarely on the head of House Speaker Gus Muetscher.

My timing wasn't the best either. I was to head the annual Austin Headliners' Club roasting of Texas politicos the very day after the news of Sharpstown had broken. The Headliners' stag luncheon had become a traditional vehicle for verbally tarring and feathering our state's political leaders as well as many national celebrities—all in good, clean, sadistic fun, you understand.

I have learned the hard way that dealing in topical political humor is like selling popsicles in Presidio. You're dealing with a perishable product. The day before I was to speak to a large gathering of Congressmen in Washington, the Abscam scandal broke. A large number of the principals involved were to be in my audience. Discard ad libs. Frantically rewrite.

The Brilab fiasco broke even as I was on a plane bound to Washington to roast a similar Congressional audience, including some of the culprits just named. Appropriately, I was rewriting my script on airsickness bags. If I'd been a Roman during the days of Julius Caesar I would have been scheduled to emcee a testimonial banquet for Brutus the day he did the old boy in.

What made the Headliners' affair so difficult was the fact that many of the men involved, in innuendo or fact, would be in my audience and were my friends. I don't mind inserting the needle, but into a still bleeding wound? I was in a dilemma.

It was then that I received a phone call from Governor Preston Smith, a friend.

"Cactus," the Governor always surprised you by calling you direct rather than using his secretary, "this is Preston. I wonder if I could come over to your office and talk to you about the Headliners' party tomorrow?"

The Governor wants to come to MY office to see me? He's going to ask me to call off the dogs sure as Bobby Layne.

"Well, Governor," I replied, "you're a lot busier than I am. I'll be glad to drop by your office."

"I sure would appreciate it, Cactus," said Governor Smith.

The Governor's office in the State Capitol building is as impressive as the granite structure in which it is housed. Even in the comfortable, casual presence of Preston Smith, you were a bit awed in that office that does not deserve such awe. I did not relish the prospect of having to tell the Governor of Texas no to his request to go easy on him.

"Cactus, I appreciate your coming," Governor Smith said with his delightful sincerity. "I'll get right to the point. About this Headliners' thing tomorrow . . ."

I said, "Yes, Governor?" Tremble, tremble.

"You're going to roast my ass about this Sharpstown thing, aren't you?" The Governor had spoken my lines for me.

"Yes, Governor, I am."

"Well, you've got to," he continued. "It's expected of you. But would you do me a favor? Would you write me a rebuttal?" he asked.

Had I been Italian I would have hugged him.

Leaving the Governor's office, I immediately called up my funny friend John Henry Faulk for a gag-writing session. We often collaborate on political scripts.

The house was packed with Romans, lions, Christians, and electricity when the Headliners' luncheon began the next day. Roast beef was served but Sharpstown was the entree. Governor Smith walked to the microphone following his introduction and began with these words: "Let he who is without stock cast the first rock." There was a frightening second of silence and then an explosion of laughter heard all the way to Amarillo. The Governor had released the pressure valve and the laughter flowed like the magic that it is. This was not the first time a politician has used the Bible to get out of trouble.

Funny Governors

Texas humor has not yet left the frontier. It is still rough and ribald, not far removed from a scorpion placed in an unsuspecting boot or a cockleburr under a saddle blanket. It is still designed to shock. This proclivity is evident in our most accomplished humorists such as Larry L. King, Dan Jenkins, and John Henry Faulk. It's reflected in our governors. We've had some funny governors in Texas, and then we've had some governors who were funny.

Price Daniel was one governor who could be funny on purpose. I became enamored with political humor when I first saw Governor Daniel and Austin lawyer St. John Garwood fight a fun duel with words before the Headliners' Club of Austin. Their preparation was a rather lengthy stay at the bar. Then before the stag audience they slugged it out with raw wit, most of it politically oriented. Not a ghostwriter's gag in the whole bunch.

When it fell my lot to emcee these annual Headliners' bloodlettings featuring our Texas governors and imported VIPs, the sessions took on a little more structure. We weren't as honest as Daniel and Garwood were. We wrote our ad libs in advance and depended on more than the bartender for help. Although I did solicit his aid before taking on Governor Allan Shivers. To kid this governor, it takes more than courage. He looks like a governor, he talks like a governor. He is the type of man you'd call mister even if you were the elder. You also kept it clean with Governor Shivers, even at a stag roast. I'd seen him react to off-color material. So I cut jokes that I'd tell a Baptist preacher but not that Methodist governor. Not that he was without humor. His humor was just suave for a Texan. Sometimes the Governor suaved himself right over the heads of his audience.

It was easier to kid Governor John Connally. He brought a lot of grist to the mill. He'd make fun of himself and would hurl a barb back at you like a chicken farmer chunking rocks at a skunk. The late humorist Morris Frank of Houston and I once worked Governor John over pretty thoroughly at a Houston banquet. When the Governor took the rostrum, he looked at Morris on his left and me on his right and quipped, "I feel like a piece of bread between two slices of ham."

Governor Preston would come to the Headliners' bash loaded with the stories that he collects wherever they are found: in the barnyard, in the cow lot, in the men's room, wherever. He's a good storyteller who collects funny stories like most politicians collect campaign contributors. I've cringed at his delivery of some of the one-liners that had been written for him. It was like Ferlin Huskey singing grand opera.

Then came Governor Dolph. Mr. Briscoe was a bonanza for us gag writers—the Chicken Ranch episode, his fondness for ranch life as opposed to mansion life, cogovernor Janey. The governor showed up for the first Headliners' luncheon during his term and left in the middle of it. I don't think Governor Dolph ever understood the kid-the-politicians games invented by the likes of Mark Twain and perfected by Will Rogers. He is too thin-skinned for the skin-piercers. He actually blushed at the tacky words. You suspected that he was hearing some of them for the first time.

I asked Governor Clements one day what he thought of the likes of us who make fun of him both from the platform and in print. He said, "Well, at first I didn't like it. But then I realized that it is part of the game and now I kinda enjoy it." He doesn't enjoy it enough to attend the Headliners' roasters, however. He professes never to tell a joke, but he has wit. I caught up with him at a banquet in Dallas. My plane was due to leave Love Field at 10:50 p.m. It was ten o'clock when I finally got to introduce him.

"Governor," I said into the microphone, "I have two

introductions here. One is for use if you will give me a ride back to Austin in your plane tonight. The other one is for use if you won't give me a ride back."

"Use the first one," retorted the Governor. "I've heard your tacky introductions before."

I got my ride home in the governor's plane, and we told each other dog stories all the way.

Spreading It Generously Around

As one who earns the gravy portion of his income on the speaking circuit, I have learned to expect the unexpected. I have experienced enough late airplanes to devise a means of coping with this frustration. I merely go into the men's room, deposit a dime for privacy, and have a nice, quiet cry.

Hecklers, I can handle. Experience will out. But I once followed the presentation of a chamber of commerce "Citizen of the Year" award given posthumously to the wife of the only recently deceased awardee. She and the entire audience were in tears while the toastmaster introduced me as "a very funny guy." I was about as funny as an Aggie joke at an A&M reunion.

Once while addressing an extremely dignified audience (they must have been dignified, they were wearing tuxedoes and evening gowns), I heard a scream at the back of the auditorium. Then a titter began at the rear and worked its way forward like a wall of water in a west Texas *arroyo* after a cloudburst. By the time it reached me it was a roar of laughter. And right behind it came a male and female wearing ski masks—period. My flashed audience was never again recapturable by one wearing clothes.

In Hot Springs, Arkansas, just before I was to address an audience of one thousand, the entire electrical system of the hotel burned out. I sometimes *leave* my audiences in the dark, but I rarely begin that way. I suggested that the caterer cater some candles while my host called the police station. I made my remarks in flickering candlelight, speaking over a police bullhorn.

I once spent two hours with an audience that was not mine. I came to the appointed room for cocktails. I visited dutifully and pleasantly with the guests during the traditional standing orgy of inane chatter and tired feet. I seated myself in an empty chair at the head table, enjoyed my meal, and waited patiently for the emcee to introduce me. He never did. My group was in the next room.

But the biggest surprise to me and my host was in a small west Texas town at the annual chamber of commerce banquet. My host was the outgoing president of the chamber. He spent the entire afternoon with me, seeing to my comforts and showing me the town. We sat side by side at the head table that evening. He served as toastmaster and got us through the plaques and prayers and promises and then began his introduction of me as the speaker for the evening. Halfway through the introduction the man paused, cleared his throat, said "excuse me," and fell over backwards, dead. The audience of four hundred sat transfixed in our high school cafeteria auditorium as artifical respiration was attempted. No one had left when the ambulance arrived and mechanical devices were used to try to revive the man. As they carried him off the stage thirty minutes after the attack, every chair was still full.

The incoming president turned to me and said, "What do we do now?"

"We give the benediction and cut," I replied.

Five years later I returned and made the speech I hadn't given on that tragic night.

The Madisonville Caper

I was very reluctant to see my friends John Henry and Elizabeth Faulk move to Madisonville, Texas. I'll tell you why.

Once a year Madisonville, Texas, plays cowboy. It's the day of the Madisonville Sidewalk Cattleman's whingding. It is a celebration of cow ownership but non-cow owners are allowed to join in. As a matter of fact, they might find it impossible not to join in, for if you are caught wearing something besides western garb on this day, you are thrown in the hoosegow or dunked in the horse trough.

The highpoint of this day of merriment is the Sidewalk Cattleman's banquet. This is how I became involved. A number of years ago I was hired to be the speaker at that event. However, in the spirit of western hurrah, it was decided that I would come incognito—as General Hans Christoffersen, Quartermaster General of the Danish Army. My mission was to buy cattle for the Danish military. I wore a costume fashioned from my old Interstate Theatres usher uniform and embellished with my high school swimming and singing medals. No one questioned the garb or the unlikely fact that a Danish general would be coming to a small east Texas town to buy cattle and make a speech. A well-known cattle buyer provided as my escort by the banquet committee added credibility.

Through the afternoon we visited various cattle raisers buying cattle. I would admit that my only acquaintance with cattle was an occasional beef steak. My cattle buyer escort would then find an excuse to go elsewhere for a few minutes, leaving the naive Dane at the mercy of the seller. I was a bird's nest on the ground. The price of cattle in Madisonville, Texas, was suddenly zooming upwards.

One of our key targets was a county judge. We visited

his courtroom but found the court in session. We stood discreetly at the side of the room until the judge finally took notice of us.

"Gentlemen," he said, "I'm going to be tied up here for some time. If you want to see me, I'd suggest you come back later."

My cattle buyer friend replied, "Well, Judge, I've got the Quartermaster General of the Danish Army here, and he is interested in maybe buying some of your cattle."

Wherewith the judge banged his gavel and declared, "Court's dismissed. Let's go to the farm."

I hope justice administered in that judge's court was better than cattle were fed on his farm. His herd of Brahma mixbreeds was as scraggly a bunch of critters as I'd ever seen.

In my best Danish accent I said, "Mr. Judge, I want you to know that Denmark is not a wealthy country. I could not possibly pay you more than three thousand dollars a head for these cattle." That was about five times their value.

"Well, I'll tell you, General, I believe in taking care of America's friends. And you ain't one of them commie countries, are you?"

I assured him we were not.

"Well then, what the heck. I'm gonna take a lickin' and let you have them at three thousand dollars per."

Before I left the judge's ranch I had bought his herd of seventy-five cows, six of his hound dogs (we Danes wanted to see how they would work as sentry dogs), and was bidding on his daughter's pet horse.

That evening at the banquet I made the key speech as the Danish general to a room full of believing sidewalk cattlemen. Then the toastmaster revealed my true identity and detailed the cattle-buying experiences of the day with emphasis on the incident with the county judge.

The audience roared, mostly with laughter but some, like the judge, just roared. And the Faulk family always wonders why I arrive so late and leave so early when I visit them in Madisonville!

The Ballad of Billie Sol

I never won a free weekend in Ruidoso because of my horse sense. My best grades in school were in non-intellectual subjects such as physical education. My talent is athletic, as I have proven many times by excelling in my favorite sport—putting foot in mouth. If this sport ever became an Olympic event I would be the modern Jesse Owens. My best performance in my chosen event occurred at the ranch of one Lyndon B. Johnson on the heretofore-"that-day" placid waters of the Pedernales River.

Senate Majority Leader Johnson was having a little party on the front lawn for some of his good old boy and girl friends. Nothing fancy—just burgers and beer and Cutty and branch water. And to further demonstrate the casualness of the get-together, I was invited to present a program of entertainment. My price was right—one burger and two Lone Stars, and I knew a group of musicians who would work for the same wages. Texas VIPs were strewn across the ranch house lawn like the herefords feeding across the river.

Towards sundown we rang the ranch bell and the group assembled in folding chairs before the public address microphone for a little entertainment. I introduced some folk singers (Bohemians—hippies hadn't yet been invented) and a fiddle band. They seemed to be doing the right numbers, because the guests' feet were tapping in collective rhythm, and the ranch owner seemed right pleased with the proceedings.

As a matter of fact, things were going so swimmingly that I decided this would be a good opportunity to introduce my latest ballad. A horse would have had more sense.

A factor in my decision to do this particular number

was the fact that the Billie Sol Estes scandal (the first one) was at its juiciest climax. And the attorney who was representing Estes, Austin lawyer Hume Cofer, was one of the guests. My song was "The Ballad of Billie Sol Estes," done as a parody on our state song, "Texas, Our Texas." It was like blaspheming bluebonnets.

So I began to regale my audience with my "hilarious" (that's a direct quote from me) lyrics. There was encouraging laughter at first. But then it dwindled to a deafening silence. I read what was happening. They were all watching their host to see his reaction to this jester's audacity, and they immediately determined from the smoky nostrils and fiery eyes that LBJ was vastly unamused.

I knew what I was doing. I was standing there singing myself to death for a burger and two Lone Stars. But there was no retreat so I continued my swan song in the key of C—as in *c*omplete panic. I came to a verse that played on Governor John Connally, who was also in the audience. When the lyrics came from my trembling mouth like blood dripping from my jugular, Governor Connally broke out in a large, gorgeous, magnificent, stupendous, colossal, fantastic guffaw!

The audience, thus released from guilt, joined brother John and soon all were rocking in uproarious laughter. Johnson, always a believer in the will of the majority, decided to join the throng and was soon holding his sides in joyous mirth. Hallelujah! I'd been saved.

I tell you this so you will understand that if John Connally should run for pope or king or even coach of the Dallas Cowboys, he will have my unwavering support and undying loyalty.

The Cowboys and the Ladies

It was the strangest mating since Zsa Zsa Gabor dated Slim Pickens. Heinz has never seen a mixture like this. West Texas twang mingled with New England whine to fill the air with soundwaves guaranteed to clear any sinus. There was pure Bronx and French spoken as well. Levi Strauss mingled with Gloria Vanderbilt. It was hash in its purest form, and it was delicious.

The National Miss Wool pageant brought all of these ingredients together, and San Angelo, Texas, homogenized them as smoothly as home-churned butter spreads on homemade bread. The whole idea was to sell wool. Since the San Angelo area is one of the world's leaders in producing the stuff, it seemed logical to those good west Texas folks that one of the nation's largest fashion shows and beauty pageants should be held in the county seat of Tom Green County.

Therefore, annually for a number of years the fashion leaders of America came to San Angelo to show their wares and help select Miss Wool of America. I had the good fortune to emcee that pageant for a number of years, and my brother Wally produced it. The contestants came from all over the nation, having been selected in preliminary contests in their home states. They modeled all-wool creations that represented the finest work of our top designers. They also came to have fun, and the beautiful young ladies and the hard-shelled representatives of the dog-eat-dog clothing industry were treated to the unequalled west Texas hospitality. They were properly barbecued, chicken-fried, and Mexican-fooded. They visited ranches and learned firsthand where steaks came from— some hadn't known. Many boarded a horse for the first time in their lives and almost all succumbed to the charm and easy manner of the west Texas community of San Angelo.

The pageant was a doozy held in an arena where the likes of Ernest Tubb was a more likely attraction than a fashion show. But the folks came in their cowboy boots and Sunday go-to-meeting clothes, and they enjoyed. National entertainers were brought in to enhance the show, and leading personalities from show business and the fashion world served as judges.

I sang a Miss Wool song to the winner just like Bert Parks as she carried her bouquet of roses down the ramp. You would have thought it was Atlantic City instead of San Angelo, Texas. It was the cowboy and the lady—and the ladies and the cowboys loved it.

Like all fashion, the Miss Wool pageant died out. But there are still a bunch of folks in San Angelo who can saucer and blow their coffee in the fashion salons of New York City anytime they're of a mind to, and they know that Gucci is a clothes designer—not a spaghetti brand.

The Pakistani and the Republican

Have you ever wondered why Eddie Arnold, the country singer, is a Republican and why my oldest son, Paul, could speak Pakistani before he could speak English? Sure you have.

It all started when Vice President Lyndon Johnson invited President Ayub Kahn of Pakistan to his ranch on the Pedernales River of Texas. Kahn was being strongly courted by the United States at the time—a very strong leader who fairly well controlled his country's destiny. LBJ wanted to go all out to make the handsome, dapper man from Pakistan feel wanted. To that end, a Texas barbecue was planned under the historic oaks of the LBJ ranch.

The famous barbecuer, Walter Jetton, brought in his chuckwagon and set up camp next to the site to prepare the food and proper checkered-tablecloths and bales-of-hay atmosphere. Since Eddie Arnold was the world's most popular singer of western songs at the time, he was invited to provide musical entertainment for the dignitaries and guests. I was to emcee the ceremonies as well as a poolside party the evening before.

The lovely Australian singer, Diana Trask, was the featured entertainment that evening, along with a water show of synchronized swimming and expert diving in the LBJ ranch swimming pool, the one shaped like a Democratic kidney. Guests were seated at tables around the pool. The Lord, being a Democrat, cooperated by providing a beautiful, warm night with a full moon larger than a ten-gallon Stetson. It fit in perfectly with Diana Trask's rendering of "Blue Moon." We bathed her in a blue spotlight that reflected off her blue sequined gown and gorgeous red hair. Her song was hypnotizing until LBJ spotted a leaf floating in the pool in front of her and ordered a yardman to take a long rake and remove the thing during the middle of Trask's song. That's the night Diana learned to sing with her eyes closed.

The next day was made for VIP barbecues. The country air was filled with the aroma of beef and ribs and hot biscuits being cooked by the world's best. Private planes circled the sky above like flocks of turkey buzzards awaiting their turn to land on the LBJ runway. The Texans and Washingtonians and Pakistanis blended together as naturally as the hereford cattle and exotic sheep grazing across the Pedernales.

The scenario called for me to begin the program following the meal by delivering my opening remarks in pure Pakistani. I had carefully memorized my lines for weeks in advance, delivering them to my young son, Paul, as he stood captive in his crib on our patio. Then I was to present singer Eddie Arnold, who would give the audience some appropriate western songs, following which I would introduce the Vice President, who was to welcome his distinguished guest, present him a Texas sombrero, and that would be that.

But that was seldom that when LBJ was involved. Halfway through the meal he collared me and said, "Introduce me now." "But," I started to protest, and that was the length of it. Five seconds later I was welcoming President Ayub Kahn in words that puzzled both the Americans and Pakistanis, I'm afraid. I introduced LBJ, he mounted the makeshift stage, welcomed his guests, and praised Ayub Kahn, giving him a cowboy hat that Kahn dutifully put on his handsome head. President Kahn responded, then Johnson led him to a nearby golf cart and the two of them rode off into the sunset with about four hundred guests and at least as many reporters and photographers following.

I then introduced Eddie Arnold to the cattle and sheep and a few chowhounds who valued barbecue more than heads of state. And you wonder why Eddie Arnold is a Republican?

Fandanglin'

It was the first time in my life that I had been asked to audition a town. President Lyndon Johnson was entertaining the ambassadors to the United States from the Latin American countries at the Texas White House on the Pedernales. Mrs. Johnson had heard of a musical presented annually by the people of tiny Albany, Texas, near Abilene. The first family wanted to entertain their distinguished guests with a barbecue meal and some "typically Texas" entertainment. So I was asked by Liz Carpenter, the First Lady's press secretary, to check the Albany musical out.

My pilot friend, Les Ready, and I flew to the community of two thousand people expecting we knew not what. We were greeted by our hosts, Elizabeth and Bill Green, and the entire town. Schools closed, businesses shut down, milking was neglected. Everybody and their dogs—literally—showed up at the school grounds to give us an audition. I felt like St. Peter or at least Cecil B. De Mille.

Writer-director Robert Nail gave the cue, and we were treated to a sampling of the Fort Griffin Fandangle. The show was being presented each summer in their own outdoor amphitheater. It depicted the settling of the Albany area, including nearby Fort Griffin. Princeton-educated Nail, who died suddenly in 1968, described the Fandangle as "people's theater" in which every element of a dramatic production was supplied by citizens of the tiny community. They were uniquely qualified to fill the roles of cowboys, Indians, and charging cavalrymen on galloping horses. They built their own stagecoach. A rancher maintained a team of mules on his ranch to pull it. They even constructed their own calliope, which was played by an Albany rancher wearing earmuffs. The costumes, sets, lighting, choreography—all homemade.

43

Fandanglin' for President and Mrs. Johnson (standing, right rear).

We were enchanted by the audition. The Johnsons accepted our recommendation and the Fandangle was booked for the LBJ Ranch. I doubt that the original settling of the Albany area was as monumental an undertaking as was the movement of the Fandangle from Albany to Stonewall, Texas. Ward Bond would have been intimidated by such a wagon train. Not so Watt Matthews. The veteran rancher, Princeton grad (Albany has the highest percentage of Princeton graduates of any community in America), and Fandangle Association president successfully led the strangest armada of wagons, trailers, and calliopes ever seen on U.S. 283.

The cast of hundreds literally took over neighboring Fredericksburg. Corrals and stables long since deserted were put into use again. Descendants of German farmers were shaken by the sight of Indians in warpaint on their main street. They were supposed to have been finished off a long time ago.

And the Latin American ambassadors to the United States, sitting in the shade of the big oaks on the grassy banks of the Pedernales, were enthralled by the songs and daredevil horseback antics of the west Texans. There wasn't a hitch, although we had to act quickly to avert one.

LBJ, the rancher, spotted his herd of herefords across the river quite a distance upstream. He summoned a secret service man and told him to tell the cowboys to bring his cattle on down where the folks could see them. Courageously I asked White House social secretary, Bess Abell, to inform the President that the cattle were cast for one of the songs, "Herding Cattle," and it was not yet time to cue the cows. The President deferred, but Bess learned that it's easier to audition a town than to tell a President to hold his cows.

Anxious Radio

Our four children were born with a microphone in front of their mouths. During our whelping years I was doing my morning radio broadcasts on KTBC (now KLBJ) from our home. The excuse was to "give the show that casual, at-home feeling." The purpose was to sleep a little later each morning.

When son number one, Paul, came along, his first gurglings and goos were literally broadcast. And when baby noises became words, they were heard by our listeners. Then three years later, when daughter Kerry arrived, we had a trio.

My wife avoided the microphone like I avoid okra salesmen. She correctly did not trust me nor what I might say when at the mike. My children were not so cautious. Paul and Kerry had their first fight with a large percentage of central Texas listening in. And the argument was over who would have the privilege of signing the program on the air that morning. When the theme faded under, the audience was treated to the sound of a brother and sister whaling one another with words and fists and a mother complaining that no other wife in America had to put up with such daily morning travails. I heard her use those same words later when I got into television and she hand-delivered to my office my hairpiece, which I had forgotten to bring with me.

Ten and nine years after the first two children we had Last (Don) and Fling (Dayne). They too joined me in my morning radio broadcasts from home. They too fought for the microphone. And they too garnered me a sizable radio audience with their proclivity for revealing family secrets as their mother winced in genuine pain.

"Daddy, Momma says that the man called and he's going to cut off our electricity if we don't pay the bill."

"Daddy, why did Uncle Raymond talk so funny and fall down and get sick last night?"

The kids all helped me with my commercials too. I was doing a pitch for a popular bread one morning. I'll not use names to protect the guilty. Suffice it to say, I asked one of my little darlings to take a bite of toast made from our sponsor's bread.

"What do you think of it?" I inquired hopefully.

"It tastes like dog doo-doo," was the fiendish reply.

Scratch one sponsor.

Other sponsors were not so finicky. Some even hoped the kids would say such shocking things about their products, because they were guaranteed to get the audience talking about them. The children always obliged.

"Paul, did you like the Dale Baker barbecue we had for supper last night?"

"Yes, Daddy."

"And again, where does that barbecue come from?"

"Dale Baker's donkey lays it, Daddy."

Dale Baker, bless his memory, loved it.

The microphone stayed in our children's lives. Paul and Kerry went on to their own careers in radio and television. Don now sings and drums in Kerry's band. And Dayne, it seems, talks all night long on the walkie-talkie that came with his volunteer fireman's uniform. My wife spends a lot of her time smiling, because there are no longer any family broadcasts emanating from our home.

Before Willie

They'd come into the studio bleary-eyed and sometimes a mite hungover. If you were the radio announcer
who was assigned to introduce their program, you were
concerned that they would make it on time, because you
knew that last night they played all the way to Ozona in
west Texas and the noon hour wouldn't be right without
the station's fiddle band on the air. But they always made
it, despite the flat tires, the sleet-slick roads, and the fatigue.

Every radio station had them back in the late '40's and
'50's. We called them "hillbilly bands" or "western bands"
or "fiddle bands" in those days. The one I worked with was
"Jessie James and All the Boys." Jessie was a highwayman,
all right. He spent half of his life on the highway, driving
to and from the nightly dances in their secondhand funeral parlor hearse, with the instruments and public address system riding back where the caskets used to lie.

The radio appearances brought them little or no money,
but were important as publicity for their nightly personal
appearances. They would read the cards and letters from
the friends out there in radio land, make the dedications
and acknowledge the requests, and then they would plug
their schedule for the week. "Tonight we're out at Dessau
Dancehall near Austin. Tomorrow night we're at the Cot-
tonbowl in Taylor. Want all you good folks up around
Waco to come join us at the Sons of Hermann's Hall on
Wednesday night."

The radio station staff band—in San Antonio it was
Red River Dave, in Taylor it was Jimmy Heep and the Mel-
ody Masters, Waco had Hank Thompson, Houston had
Floyd Tillman, Fort Worth had the Lightcrust Doughboys.
They were a part of our culture.

Every night the scene was the same, only the dancers changed. The wooden bandstand illuminated mostly by Pearl and Lone Star beer neon signs, the ice-slick dance floor, the long tables occupied by the city dudes and the country folks of Germanic, Slavic, or Scandinavian stock, drinking their beer or pouring from the brown bag on the table. Often the newly born baby was placed on top of the table too and friends would watch the baby while mom and pop danced. Sometimes there would be a wedding party and the band would play "The Anniversary Waltz." You'd see the bride dancing with her bridesmaids in their home-made flowing gowns while the groom stayed at the table to talk to poppa-in-law about crops and land. The band would play the Paul Jones and the Herr Schmidts and the "put-your-little foots" while everyone danced around the floor in a counterclockwise direction. Always counter-clockwise. If you knew the bandleader you could usually count on him buying you a round or two, because Pearl or Lone Star gave him a little budget to plug their products.

On Saturday nights when it was so crowded there wasn't room enough for the smoke, there would be a fight or two. But this was part of the routine, so the constable was there drinking his beer with the best of them, waiting to take control when it came time for him to go to work. Then after the dance, the band would load up the hearse, and check the tires for flats and the dancehall for any girls who might have lingered. Tomorrow night, the same songs, mostly in the key of C or F, and "keep them cards and letters coming in, friends and neighbors out there in radio land."

One Moment, Please

Lauritz Melchior, star of grand opera and motion pictures, was seated across the table from me, a microphone in between us.

"Mr. Melchior, it's a gawd damn pleasure to have you on my show."

The big Danish tenor blushed a tomato red and stammered, "Vell, uh, vell, it's a pleasure to be vith you also."

"Mr. Melchior," I continued, "I hear that you have recently been to Africa and shot an elephant that was a big sonavabitch."

"Vell, I vould not exactly put it in those terms, but yah, he was a big von alright," blurted my startled guest.

What I was doing, of course, was using a hidden button to clip the profane words that had brother Melchior thinking that he was being interviewed by a madman—as perhaps he was.

From that same KTBC radio studio in Austin I once hid five different alarm clocks set to go off at five different times during the next fifteen minutes. During that period our news editor Paul Bolton attempted to deliver a newscast. The audience never knew why bells were ringing during Paul's news that day and why he sounded so angry. And without even making inquiry, the man had the audacity to accuse *me* of perpetrating the devious deed!

Dirty tricks used to be an integral part of the broadcast game. We used to delight in figuring out practical jokes to play on our fellow broadcasters. It doesn't happen in modern broadcasting. News departments are saving the dirty tricks for the newsmakers, and I suspect that senses of humor have changed not for the better.

Bob Gray, news editor of KNUZ in Houston when I was working there, had a sense of humor, or I would not be here to relate that fact. He would dash into the studio just seconds before his fifteen-minute noon newscast, assemble his notes, and prepare to read his daily report. Quite frequently, something would "just happen" to go wrong with the lights and Bob would be left in a studio as black as a cave and only his memory between him and his audience. To the man's credit, the audience never had a clue. He would deliver fifteen minutes of news in total darkness without a single stammer.

Bob Gray was not without a sense of vengeance. One day he "just happened" to be ill. I was asked to substitute for him on his newscast. Smelling a rat—and being a very clever fellow—I set up to do the news from another studio where the light switch was within my reach. As I smugly began my newscast in full lighting, a beautifully dressed, well-endowed woman came and sat quietly across the table from me. She removed her hat. She removed her gloves. When she removed her blouse, she got some of my attention. When she removed her brassiere, she got the rest of it, and my news copy got none. You can't believe how long a fifteen-minute newscast can be until you've broadcast one with a totally nude woman sitting across the desk from you. And you also can't believe how shocked a station manager can be when he glances into a studio and sees his newscaster delivering the news to a nude woman.

Of course Bob Gray and his chortling cohorts had hired a stripper for their classic act of revenge. I was so flustered I didn't attempt another practical joke for almost twenty-four hours.

Countrifyin' Houston

"Country" was not invented at Gilley's in Houston, Texas. There were urban cowboys long before John Travolta did his Marlon Brando mumblings over a long-necked bottle of Lone Star. I'm proud to say that I had a hand in chicken-frying cosmopolitan Houston.

It was in 1947. Network radio was in its heyday. Can you believe a world without "All in the Family" reruns? Walter Cronkite didn't even know what it was that was to be the way that it is. Evenings at home were dominated by Bob Hope, Bing Crosby, the Lux Radio Theatre, One Man's Family, Fibber McGee and Molly, and that improbable duo for radio, Charlie McCarthy and Edgar Bergen.

A couple of World War II veterans turned Houston advertising men, Max Jacobs and Doug Hicks, bought the radio frequency that Judge Roy Hoffheinz, the father of the Astrodome, was vacating in order to move his station to a different and more powerful frequency. He spent a fortune promoting the move. Hicks and Jacobs gave one of their employees, Thelma Bradshaw, a casual little assignment of putting a radio station on the air. She assembled a crew of World War II veterans of the Battle of Britain and Sheppard Field, Texas, including Dave Morriss as manager and me as program manager. Our budget wouldn't buy a shoestring. We were—and they still are—KNUZ.

The first question ownership threw at us was, "How are we going to combat the big network nighttime shows with no network?"

"Simple," sez we. "We bring in country music disc jockeys like Biff Collie (now a member of the Country Music Hall of Fame) and Walter Colvin and hit 'em with 'The Houston Hoedown.'"

"What's a hoedown?" follows Jacobs.

"Lunatics! You can't play country music in sophisticated, citified Houston, Texas. Man, we're uptown, have private clubs that serve mixed drinks and cafes that feature steaks that are not fried. This ain't no hick town!" said Mr. Hicks.

"No," we replied, "but it's a town full of hicks who will get their kicks with Roy Acuff and Tennessee Ernie."

We hit the air that first night with Nashville's best going against the cream of Hollywood and New York City. We asked the friends and neighbors out there in radio land to call in their requests. We also confessed that we were poor boys and could sure use some food and free entertainment passes and free cleaning and pressing—whatever the good people out there could spare. One hour later the manager of the telephone company interrupted one of the calls to inform us that the traffic flow was so heavy we were disrupting their entire system. So we asked our audience to write in their requests and dedications. Within twenty-four hours we had around five thousand letters and enough food, passes, and other handouts to support ourselves to the shaky payday we hoped was but two weeks away. Poverty the people could relate to.

Our salesmen divided the five thousand letters up into five boxes, descended upon the Houston advertising agencies, and dumped their whole boxload on the time buyers' desks with the declaration, "There are ten thousand letters there. Count 'em. Now how about buying some time on our little ol' radio station?" Within two weeks we were sold out and the little underdog was beating the pants off the Houston network stations, including Judge Hoffheinz's.

We didn't break the mold with KNUZ. We made the mold. We introduced the singing station breaks to the city, homemade (God, please don't let me die with that as my main contribution to mankind). We taught Houston that "D.J." stood for something besides "dig jalapeños."

We even dared to program a Black man, Lonnie Rochon,

"the King Bee," playing rhythm and blues records on a white man's station. That uncovered a relatively untapped market of two hundred thousand fans of Black rhythm and blues, as well as every redneck bigot who could crawl out from under his rock. We were bombarded with threats —and inundated with advertisers wanting to testify to their newly found love of their Black brethren. Larry went on to become the driving force in creating Black radio in America.

Floyd Tillman and Little Marge, Leon Payne, whose career was launched from this station with "I Love You Because," and other country stars performed live from our studio. We took "The Houston Hoedown" on the road and originated live from Cook's Hoedown Club. Houston, Texas, done took the country music boys to their little ol' citified hearts. And all this long before electric bulls had ever been invented or Bum Phillips had a cowboy hat. Ahhh ha!

The Law South of the Belt

I don't know who Alice was, but had she known the town when I was living there she would have changed her name.

Alice, Texas, is located about 35 miles south of Corpus Christi, 15 miles from Kingsville, and, back in the '40's, a light-year or two from law and order.

Jim Wells County is where they put her, snuggled up to Duval County just as comfortably as Bonnie to Clyde. The Duke of Duval, George Parr, was the "papacito" of this area occupied predominantly by Mexican-Americans. He ran things in the good old democratic way—poverty was evenly distributed among the have-nots and wealth was evenly distributed among the Parr family and their political cronies.

Papa Parr controlled the area like Willie Nelson controls audiences. He could get it done if he liked you, and he could get you done if he didn't. The fact that he controlled the votes of Jim Wells and Duval counties is legend—from cradle to the grave (and there were tabulated voters from both sources).

I hit Alice, Texas, in 1946 as program director of radio station KBKI so blissfully ignorant that I thought a Parr was something that eluded you on the golf course. I later learned that you weren't safe from Parr's reach even on the golf course.

Our station was not the ordinary radio station operation. For two things, we had two managers in enthusiastic opposition to each other. The host of our mid-afternoon Mexican-language broadcast was paid just $400 a month. Yet somehow he managed a new Cadillac for himself and one for his wife, plus expensive clothes, diamond rings, and other luxuries unknown to those of our profession.

Once I opened one of his hundreds of daily letters by mistake. A dollar bill fell out. Another letter contained a five-dollar bill. We checked and discovered that Juan Dinero was charging $1 for musical requests, $2 for wedding announcements, and $5 for funeral announcements. The John D. Rockefeller of Tortilla Flat!

Management reacted by demanding half the loot and hiring a Spanish-speaking person to monitor our Latin friend's broadcasts.

Another oddity of our radio station was our involvement with local news. You ever tune in the six o'clock news and hear the newsman say, "Hey! Guess what? Our local deputy sheriff is condoning prostitution and importing professional softball pitchers and boarding them in the county jail so they can pitch for the sheriff's team in the city tournament"? Our news editor Mike Holberg laid that one on our audiences one day. It was the hottest news to hit Alice since they lost Box #13, which contained the eighty-seven votes that put Lyndon Johnson in the U.S. Senate and Coke Stevenson back by the campfire.

The following day Holberg and I were playing golf on Alice's scenic seven-hole version of St. Andrews. Following the slicing ball with my eyes, I saw a battleship approaching us from the Gulf of Mexico thirty-two miles away. No, it wasn't a battleship. Battleships don't wear Stetsons and carry pearl-handled six-shooters on their hips.

Could it be? Yes it was. Deputy Sheriff Sam Smithwick and his entire 275 pounds and six feet four inches all fettled with MAD.

"Are you those two radio guys who put that story about me on the air?"

"Mike Holberg here is our news editor," I volunteered, never one to take credit away from a colleague.

"You guys have got 'til sundown to get out of town."

Republic Pictures surely had a copyright on that line, used in every single one of the western movies they ever produced.

We checked in with the "owner" of the radio station,

Alice attorney Ed Lloyd, and laughingly told him of our encounter with the sheriff in the rough.

"Boys," he said (and we were), "let me give you a few facts of life. Who do you think put Smithwick in office? And who do you think really controls this radio station?"

Magically the name Parr came into our minds, and we weren't thinking Jack.

"Take my advice, and don't wait until sundown to leave."

Mike was gone by two p.m., and my wife and I were setting up housekeeping in Corpus Christi by 3:30 that afternoon.

The man who succeeded me as program director at KBKI was Bill Mason. He too broadcast some tacky remarks about Deputy Sheriff Smithwick. Mason was sitting in his automobile one lazy afternoon on the main street of Alice. Smithwick walked up to him and shot him to death.

Smithwick later committed suicide in a Bell County jail. And I became devotedly committed to a life of cowardice.

Antique Television

The first words I spoke before a television camera were, "What did you expect, hair?" I had been a hairless radio announcer. But there had been no reason to let the audience in on that truth. Television reveals all. That was thirty years ago, and I suddenly find myself a veteran in the new industry that has revolutionized the world. I have been no shining light in that revolution—hardly an ember. We did what had to be done without knowing how to do it, and we had a lot of fun.

All of my television years have been with KTBC television in Austin. I started out as program manager simply because I was program manager of KTBC radio. Why waste two name plaques and two desks? When we began, our studio was a very small glassed-in booth within the confines of the transmitter building. The cameras peered through a plate glass window at the performers inside. Everything was live, for there was no videotape. One of my first programming decisions was to utilize two newscasters, Paul Bolton and Lyman Jones, on the same newscast. "A shocking waste of talent," shouted the accounting department. "Video variety," was my rebuttal. If there was a live commercial during the newscast, the announcer who delivered it had to literally crouch beneath the desk from which the newscasters delivered their news. With the words "and now a word from our sponsor," up would pop the announcer (usually me) to deliver his pitch. Pitch concluded, he would sink down out of sight until needed.

Technically, television has progressed tremendously during these thirty years. I can't say the same about programming. *Laverne and Shirley* remains a step below *Howdy Doody* in my opinion—as do most of the current mess of sitcoms that have been sifted down to the lowest level of mediocrity. But the technical boys have done their jobs and it's reflected in the superior coverage of sporting events and worldwide news.

At the beginning, as I said, we were dangerously live. If you said it, they heard it—and saw you say it. No magic button to push to put the words back in your mouth. In our makeshift studio within our transmitter building, if the lights behind the cameras were left on, the camera would pick up a reflection off the window that separated the performers from the cameras. During one show the door to the john, which was located right behind the camera area, accidentally swung open to reveal one of our newscasters sitting on his throne. Some said his finest television moment.

We made do. The first television show I hosted was *Cacti's Fill Time*. And that's exactly what it was—a show to fill the time when there was nothing else to program or when the network or film camera failed to function. I would play records with hand puppets for exciting video, read letters, interview anyone who was within grabbing distance, and literally fill time.

A daily live television show with no rehearsal time and only two cameras was something akin to doing a daily parachute jump without a parachute. In both cases the end result was usually the same. But we invented a safety net. We personalized the cameras—named them Ralph and Fappy Lou. We painted eyes on them, put a bonnet and a bow on Fappy Lou, and talked to them. The cameras became television personalities. They received fan mail. If Fappy Lou fouled up a shot, she was ordered by the emcee to go stand in the corner. The audience would see a shot of the camera being pushed to the corner of the studio and then there would be a shot of the corner. When we asked our two electronic stars questions, they would respond affirmatively by tilting up and down or negatively by panning from side to side.

Corny stuff? No, ingenious make-doism. When we later moved our studios downtown into the southeast ground floor of the historic Driskill Hotel we introduced what might have been the best idea for a television show ever devised. We called it "Street Scene." We simply opened the doors to Sixth and Brazos, played good music, and let the cameras photograph the people passing by. It was people-watching at its best. Alas, the show was cancelled when a masked flasher raised the show's rating to "R." He also caused our switchboard to be flooded with calls from women wanting to know who he was and where he could be reached.

Naturally, there was a country music show. Ours was the *TV Dude Ranch*—the *Gong Show* without tongue in cheek. We were in the big time now. Real sets—a barnyard with shiny concrete floor, a brick fireplace with glowing coals in the middle of July. One Christmas season we even introduced falling snow during the rendering of an appropriate song. Ingeniously, we used Ivory Soap Flakes for snowflakes. It was a little hot in the studio for snow, however. Hot enough to make the singer, Max Garner, wet with perspiration. And the moisture combined with the soap soon produced a very sudsy singer blinded by the stuff filling his eyes. First case of indoor snow blindness ever recorded.

Early live television had its moments—like the weatherman who forgot to zip up, or a guest herpetologist on the Uncle Jay Show who dropped and broke an aquarium full of snakes in a studio full of children whose parents were watching from the viewing room above. And then there was the day that my co-host Jean Boone and I got tickled trying to say the dangerous words "Smucker's Jelly" and the camera would not go away as we doubled up in laughter for five continuous, torturous minutes.

Primitive television? Perhaps, but there were advantages—such as no reruns.

Hints about Heloise

I knew there was something about this woman that was different. Something you couldn't quite put your finger on—an aura? A mystique?

And then I realized what it was. Her hair was green. Not your normal shade of green, mind you, but avocado green with just a dash of the Notre Dame color. When I complimented her dress I perceived that this woman did not fit the mold of normalcy. She told me that she had purchased it off a woman whom she had encountered on the street. She liked the dress, so she bought it right then and there—swapping hers for the woman's.

The late Heloise Cruse was no ordinary woman. The native Texan, who went on to become the world's most widely read columnist with her hints to housewives, was the greatest spot remover in history. (Her daughter now continues the column, "Here's Heloise.") Her passion in life was telling the world's housewives how to get spots off their glassware and remove lipstick stains from their husband's collars.

I was dining in her apartment one evening and accidentally turned my glass of wine over on the beautifully embroidered tablecloth. I was embarrassed, but Heloise was delighted. It gave her the opportunity to test out one of her new hints: How to remove wine from a tablecloth. She poured wax from the candelabra on the stain. It worked.

I was in the Cruses' Washington apartment to record a series of radio broadcasts with Heloise for international syndication. We had tried doing the pilots in a Washington recording studio complete with scripts. But Heloise, we soon learned, had no household hints on how to suc-

Taking a hint from Heloise Cruse.

cessfully read household hints. She was a talker, not a reader. So we shifted gears and tried ad-libbing the shows.

Heloise had many talents. And one of them was the ability to speak 15 minutes of pure profanity and never once repeat a word. As co-host I'd ask Heloise how to clean a toilet bowl. She'd give me the right answer, but she spoke in language a bit too explicit for public broadcast. And so it went.

Finally, the dynamic lady decided that the atmosphere was wrong—that she needed to be in her own kitchen to do the show properly. So we moved to her flat with all the recording equipment. We had almost as much equipment as the control tower of the Washington National Airport, which, unfortunately, was only a tad more than a dab away. The roar of planes overhead in the sound engineer's earphones made his eyes roll like cherries in a runaway slot machine.

Still, Heloise insisted that this was the only place where she could work. So we improvised a studio—in her storage closet. We lined the walls with blankets. Still the sound of the planes bled through. We tried different microphones. No luck. Finally, Heloise came up with another one of her famous household hints. If you want to keep out the sound of airplanes from your storage closet, drape a blanket over your head.

And that's literally what we did for a week—sat in Heloise's closet and recorded interviews with a blanket over our heads. We got five shows, and the engineer collected about five miles of taped profanities that would make a good gift for your favorite enemy. I got a beautiful conversation starter: Did I ever tell you about the time I spent a week under a blanket with Heloise?

In the Big Bend Country with the White House Press Corps.

Buckshot Bean

Did I ever tell you of the time Judge Roy Bean got me into trouble? It all began when First Lady Lady Bird Johnson and United States Secretary of the Interior Stuart Udall led a band of semi-intrepid, mostly female members of the White House Press Corps on a tour of the Big Bend country of Texas—probably as revenge for the years of journalistic sniping.

The junket included a tour of historic Fort Davis and the dedication of that colorful relic as a National Historic Site. This was followed by a trip down the Rio Grande through beautiful Mariscal Canyon in rafts carrying the most bizarre assortment of passengers since the Love Boat took on the Muppets. Lady Bird and Secretary Udall led the way. They were followed by the likes of Liz Carpenter, Helen Thomas, Shana Alexander, and Nancy Dickerson on-the-rocks. And I might add, over the rocks, in between the rocks, and sometimes under the rocks. It seems as if I spent more time in the water than on it, pulling Washington reporter Isabelle Shelton out of the drink. Obviously she had not majored in white water journalism. Politicians would have loved the sight of the infamous poison pen gals being dashed against boulders and drenched in the chilly April waters of the Rio Grande. Some were unflappable, however. There was one lady dressed as if attending a garden party in Victorian England. Constantly above her head was a pink parasol. That parasol became our flag; as long as it waved there was life.

At the end of the day-long journey, I gave thanks for surviving the ordeal, pleasurable and exhilarating as it was. But the greatest danger lay ahead, I later learned. Mrs. Johnson's press secretary, Liz Carpenter, is the notorious female villain of role casting (she has cast me in the roles of a tree, a yellow highway center stripe, Christopher Columbus on a trip to Texas, and the father of eight noisy children). On the night of a campfire in the Big Bend for the Fourth Estate, she decided that it would be high entertainment if I were to appear as Buckshot Bean, nephew of Judge Roy Bean, the famous Law West of the Pecos.

The site was high atop a mountain. Glowing campfires aided by the traditional Washington bottled remedies warded off the chill of the starry night. The spirits of Indian braves were frightened off by the voices of White House reporters singing campfire girl songs.

I left the scene to retire to my cabin almost a mile down the trail. There I donned my disguise as Buckshot Bean— a huge beard, a large floppy western hat, a tattered leather vest, and sadly worn boots and trousers. I looked like a cross between Gabby Hayes and John L. Lewis. I carried an ancient rifle under my arm, and with the other arm I led a jackass. That made two of us.

I made my way slowly up the dark and somewhat treacherous trail toward the campfire, frequently stumbling and muttering words not fit for Liz Carpenter's ears. As I rounded a bend nearing the campfire, suddenly a round piece of metal tried to go through my stomach. It was a pistol barrel, on the other end of which was a secret service agent.

"Drop that gun!" he commanded.

It dropped.

"Now where do you think you're going?"

"To the bathroom unless you get that pistol out of my stomach," I gasped.

Liz Carpenter with her great attention to detail had not informed the Secret Service of the almost late Buckshot Bean. When summoned she came to my rescue, but the campfire performance that followed was not nearly as memorable as the one that had preceded as the descendant of the Law West of the Pecos met the real law east of the Pecos.

The White House on the Pedernales

All of a sudden it dawned on me. That was the President of the United States and the Chancellor of Germany, with the key members of their cabinets, walking into the room where I was waiting.* Erhard of Germany and Johnson of America. If my hands had not been trembling so, I would have pinched myself to make sure it was true.

The two leaders and their department heads had been enjoying a stag dinner in the adjoining room of the LBJ ranch. It was LBJ's first such function for a visiting head of state—only weeks after the assassination of President Kennedy. I had been asked to provide some entertainment for the evening. The State Department folks had told me that Erhard was a musicologist, so I obtained a string quartet from the Austin Symphony to provide background music during the dinner. I then suggested a beautiful blonde singer from Fort Worth, Linda Loftis, who had been a finalist in the Miss America competition and had won the talent category. The State Department eyebrows could be heard arching across the room at the suggestion that a beauty contest winner be used for such an august assemblage. But once they heard Linda's magnificent classical voice and viewed her stunning beauty you would have thought that Secretary of State Dean Rusk had personally requested her. Her accompanist was Ezra Rachlin, conductor of the Austin Symphony.

The dinner apparently had gone well. LBJ did send word out to me a time or two to have the string quartet play something peppy like "Yellow Rose of Texas" or "Don't Fence Me In." I assured him that unless those songs had been authored by Brahms or Bach, they wouldn't know them.

*December 29, 1963

After the meal, the distinguished guests and hosts wandered into the large comfortable living room for cigars and brandy and entertainment. I made my opening remarks as emcee in rapidly memorized German delivered with a south Austin accent. The rotund chancellor raised his glass and toasted me for my "fine command of the Italian language."

I then introduced Linda. With her blonde hair and blue eyes she looked more Berlin than Fort Worth. And as she performed her program of German leider songs in flawless German, one German diplomat suggested that we had brought in a ringer from the old country. The audience, especially the Germans, was transfixed.

As Linda was singing, I glanced toward the porch window. Peeking through the panes like a child spying on Santa Claus on Christmas Eve was Lady Bird Johnson. Not even first ladies are allowed at stag parties.

Linda sang one Italian opera aria that evening. As she concluded, the beaming chancellor stood and took a yellow rose from a nearby vase and handed it to Linda, saying, "How did you know that was my very favorite aria?"

Then the German Secretary of State stood. "Gentlemen, I would like to tell you a true story. Many years ago in Berlin I attended the debut of a twelve-year-old German boy pianist. It was one of the most remarkable performances I had ever enjoyed. I had often wondered what had happened to him. Tonight I have found the answer. That pianist is the man who has been accompanying Miss Loftis—Maestro Ezra Rachlin."

Mary Martin

I once had dinner with Mary Martin. How's that for name-dropping? But it's true. However, I should add that there were about thirty or forty other Martin fans there as well. At our table of eight, I proposed a toast—a toast to me—because I was the lucky guy who got to sit next to Mary Martin for an entire meal—and that's a toastable happening.

I wasn't very nervous. I always try to cut my steak with my spoon just to test the tenderness, and I always pour cream into my water glass—it forms such interesting patterns swirling in the water. I was cool. I successfully avoided the cliché questions like: What is J.R. really like? Do you miss being on Broadway? No, I hit her with an original one: Have you ever been to Austin before? She had.

But she came to my rescue. It soon became apparent that Mary Martin is for real and as comfortable as a hammock full of houseshoes. As a matter of fact, it was she who brought up the subject of what her son "J.R." (Larry Hagman) is really like. And what he's like, according to his adoring mother, is a lot of fun. She told of the time when they were together in Las Vegas. Upon leaving the hotel he was swarmed with autograph seekers who ignored her. As the limousine pulled away with the adoring fans running after it, J.R. turned to his mother and said, "Well, Ma, that's show biz." From there they went to one of the hotels to catch Joel Grey entertaining. In the middle of his act, Grey stopped and acknowledged the presence of his old friend and neighbor, Larry Hagman. Hagman stood to good applause. Then Grey said, "And now I'd like to introduce Larry's mother—a woman I've never met but whom I admire as much as anyone in the business—Mary Martin."

Well, Mary Martin had experienced as much applause as any American entertainer—but she related that this was among the most thunderous standing ovations she had ever received. When the din finally died down, she turned to her son, J.R., and said, "No, THAT'S show biz."

After dinner we retired to our hostess' living room for some old-fashioned song-singing and storytelling. I urged the pianist to move casually into one of the songs from *South Pacific*. It worked. The lady loves her craft and soon Mary Martin was enthralling a room full of guests dizzy with the knowledge that they were witnessing one of the great ladies of show business in a private performance. Actually, it was not a performance. She was merely joining in the spirit of the evening. She was one of us. And that's the beauty of this still beautiful lady. There is nothing pretentious about her—a very natural person.

She lives in Palm Springs now and still makes an occasional appearance on some of the television talk shows. She finds it painful to return to her ranch home in Brazil—too many memories of happy days there with her late husband. She remains a Texan in spirit and in soul, the little gal from Weatherford whom Billy Rose turned down for a role in a musical at Fort Worth's Casa Mañana. He recalled that goof one night in introducing her at a New York banquet honoring her.

And just for the record, she may be sixty-nine years old, but there are few women that age who distract me to the point of trying to eat my soup with my fork—which I did that night.

Van Cliburn's Barn Dance

Perhaps you wonder why Van Cliburn gives me indigestion. The brand-new President of the United States, Lyndon Johnson, was entertaining the Chancellor of Germany, Ludwig Erhard, and his cabinet at his ranch on the Pedernales River of central Texas. The whole world was watching Johnson. They were curious as to what his style would be. His predecessor had been dead but for a short while, and the Kennedy image still shown brightly.

Naturally, a Texas barbecue was planned. Liz Carpenter, Mrs. Johnson's press secretary, and Bess Abell, White House social secretary, huddled with me regarding entertainment for the affair. I suggested that it might be a good opportunity to demonstrate to the world that Texas was not just fiddle bands. Why not have our most famous classical musician, pianist Van Cliburn, perform under the big oak trees that shade the herefords grazing on those grassy banks? They concurred and we called Van's mother. They accepted our invitation.

The dozens of administrative assistants who specialize in outdoor worry put their administrative heads together and concluded that the barbecue should be held indoors; not knowing Texas, they feared rain. The site was moved to the Stonewall school gymnasium across the river and down the road apiece from the LBJ ranch. Other administrative types in charge of indoor worry gave out instructions that no word was to be released about Cliburn's appearance. But when an enterprising reporter saw them removing an entire side of the Stonewall gymnasium in order to move in a concert grand piano, he concluded that Floyd Cramer was not the man who would serenade the two heads of state. He soon put two and two together and got Cliburn.

I was in the middle of my television show one day when the floor manager held up a sign reading "Cut. Emergency." Suspecting an open fly, I broke for commercials and the long-distance telephone call awaiting me in the control room. It was Mrs. Cliburn calling from Shreveport. The local editor had called her and informed her that Van was going to be playing at a *barn dance* in a country school. Her purpose in calling was to inform me that no way was her son to play for a barn dance, even if the Chancellor of Germany was dancing with the President of the United States.

Visions of headlines raced through my throbbing head: "Van Cliburn's Mother Says LBJ Tries to Make Hillbilly Out of Her Son," "Van Cliburn Shuns Texas Hayseeds," "Kennedys Titter as LBJ Burns."

"Mrs. Cliburn," I stammered, "please don't do a thing for fourteen minutes and twenty-two seconds. That's how long I have to go on my television show. I'll call you right back."

Fortunately it was not color television. My green face would have frustrated the viewing audience trying to adjust their sets. As soon as I signed off, I got Mrs. Cliburn back on the phone and assured her that even though the setting was a gymnasium and even though there were checkered tablecloths and bales of hay stacked around for atmosphere, her son would not be playing for a barn dance.

She simmered and I shivered and Van played and wowed the Germans as Texas put its best classical foot forward. But I still get indigestion every time I hear a Van Cliburn recording.

Mad Mondays

The hostesses on the flight to Dallas, who are usually so friendly and frisky, could have been deputy constables serving me a summons from their manner. First time I've ever been told to "fasten your seat belt or get out, buster." The passengers seemed to have inherited their mood, somber and surly. I asked the occupant of 3A—I was 3C— if I could read the newspaper that he had just put down between us on 3B. "If you want a newspaper, buy it!" was the response.

Even the flower children at the airport hawking their religious publications and generally seeking loot scowled at me when I gave them a pleasant, "Good morning."

There was a vacant cab at the curb. "Is this cab available?" I asked the driver.

"Do you think I'm parked here because I like the panoramic view of the parking lot?" he snapped. "Get in and tell me where you want to go."

The streets were filled with madmen. Cars were cutting in front of each other like mullets being chased by hungry mackerel. Brakes were screeching, horns were blasting, drivers were sticking their heads out the windows hurling profanities at one another. For a moment I thought I had taken the wrong plane and was in New York City rather than Dallas. I saw a traffic policeman pull a little old lady through the window of her car for sassing him, and she began beating him on the head with his billy club. Dogs were not only chasing cars; they were catching them and biting the tires.

At the hotel I asked the doorman to please take my luggage inside. He said, "Take it yourself, Mac. I didn't take you to raise."

He really got irritable when I refused to tip him.

The hotel clerk was asleep with his head on the registration book, a badly spent bottle of vodka leaning against his head. I rang the bell to awaken him, and he called hotel security to report me for creating a disturbance.

The bellboy asked me if I could take only those things that I would need out of my suitcase and check the rest downstairs, so he wouldn't have to carry such a load. When I told him no, he went on strike.

My room was not made up. The television set was sitting in the bathtub, which was full of water. The window drapes and carpet appeared to have been chewed up by some monstrous machine.

I called housekeeping and asked them to send a maid to clean my room, and they called me a fascist pig. My message light was flashing, so I called the operator. She said, "The message is from me. Drop dead!"

I glanced out the window and noticed a plane skywriting. It was writing in smoke the largest four-letter profanity I had ever seen.

I tell you all this as a warning. Never go to Dallas, Texas, on a Monday morning if the Cowboys lost on Sunday afternoon.

The Deer Hunter

I suspect that deer hunting is a very fortunate thing for our Texas society. There is an army of Texans who need the whitetail and mule deer to annually assert man's mastery over the wild creatures. Frankly, I never felt myself master of nature's animals. Who's got the best deal? The men and women who spend hundreds of dollars and make all kinds of sacrifices to desert their asphalt jungles for a few weekends in the out-of-doors? Or the animals who spend their lives in that setting? Show me a whitetail buck on the Houston freeway, and I'll show you a crazy deer. Show me a covey of quail waiting for a plane to lose its mechanical difficulties at Love Field, and I'll show you birds that have been feeding on marijuana. Masters indeed!

Somewhere along the way I lost my "primitive instincts" to be a hunter. It's probably a psychological reaction to having been the hunted so often—hunted by truant officers, hunted by bill collectors, hunted by top sergeants. I've been fair game all my life. I have made field champions out of three fine Labrador retrievers and have been duck hunting but once. A pair of leaky rubber waders and a wealth of thirty-three degree water at five o'clock in the morning made me an avid duck conservationist for the rest of my life.

I have killed—excuse me—I have "harvested" deer. "Harvest" is the modern lexicon of the deerslayer. Somehow I feel that an enthusiastic hunter shouldn't sit and cry over his kill. But I do love the deer hunt. I'm as good a hunter as you will find in the cabin. I can hold my own with any pancake eater. I'll stay with the best in the hunting camp poker game. I once bagged a twelve point card-

Loaded for bear—er, deer—Cactus the mighty hunter.

shark. I'll endure the snores of a cabin full of train engines without a whimper.

In all modesty, I look the role of a hunter. I could well be heading for a filming session for Marlboro cigarettes when I don my flannel plaid shirt, my corduroy breeches, my carefully weathered Stetson 3xxx beaver. I polish my rifle with affection and finesse. My custom-made hunting knife is sharpened to a razor's edge with the deft touch of a man accustomed to using such a tool. My boots are not new from the mail catalogue. They are time- and weather-worn boots with the soil and stain of many a country mile decorating their exterior.

I'm a good getter-upper. No matter how late the festivities of the night before, no matter how early the hour, nor how cold the weather outside, I'm leading the pack to get 'em up.

"What are you, a bunch of pansies? Get outta that sack and out into the open. Those big bucks are waiting!"

As the gang grudgingly and slowly vacate the cabin, I'm still headin' 'em out like a wagonless wagon master. And as the last one steps out into the shocking cold, dark morning, the joy of deer hunting overwhelms me as I quietly climb back into my bunk, pull the covers over me, and sink into the soft, sweet arms of slumber.

Kite and Crenshaw

Austin sports fans always have a pair of aces in the hole. If the Dallas Cowboys should falter, if the Oilers should end up with a duster, if the Longhorns should come a fall cropper, there's always a light at the end of the tunnel. There's always the forthcoming golf season and there are always Ben and Tom.

The dynamic duo that grew up on the capital city's municipal and country club courses give Austinites the chance to golf vicariously around the globe. We watch Tom Kite and Ben Crenshaw, our favorite weekend golfers, as they challenge the top courses and golfers of the world. And when they're not on television we scan the previous day's scores in the newspapers like a retired banker reading yesterday's stock market reports. They've been feeding our egos for years, first as outstanding junior golfers, and later as All-Americans together on the University of Texas national collegiate championship team under Coach George Hannon. Now they feed our egos as two of the top professional golfers on the tour.

In a very real sense Tom and Ben are Austin's sons. There's a lot more than community pride in their athletic achievement; there's a community parental affection for these two hometown products with their good manners, their modesty, and their continuing love of Austin. If there was a town wallet, photographs of Ben and Tom would adorn it.

But adoration of Tom and Ben is not limited to Austin, Texas. I once had the good fortune to have a day in St. Andrews, Scotland. My luck held when I found three Englishmen in search of a fourth golfer to replace an ill friend. Our caddies were all fifth, sixth, even seventh generation bag-carriers on the links where the game began in the sixteenth century. I was just another hacker to come to mecca until I casually mentioned that I knew Ben Crenshaw and Tom Kite and had come from the same city. Suddenly Mr. Hyde became Dr. Jekyl. My English companions began asking my opinion on shot-making. My ancient caddy, who up until then had uttered only one sound, "tch, tch, tch," in response to my golf game, began flooding me with his memories of the year when the two dear Texans, Kite and Crenshaw, tied for second in the British Open, played at St. Andrews. He showed me exactly where their balls lay following their tee shots on the eighteenth hole. The other caddies joined in with praise of Crenshaw's knowledge of the game of golf, its players, and its courses throughout history. And when I got lucky and birdied the final hole in front of the historic clubhouse, my seventy-five-year-old caddie's comment was, "Ah yes, laddies, just like Kite and Crenshaw." Fallout fame.

But the best reward came from my three English golfing companions. "Richard"—they could not deal with the name 'Cactus'—"Richard," they said, "we've met your Jimmy Connors and your John McEnroes. And while we admire the game of tennis they play, we're grateful to know that there are still young athletes in America with the grace and charm of Tom Kite and Ben Crenshaw."

I would have given back my birdie just to hear that.

The Arena

My mother had the good sense to bring me into this world within earshot of the cheers of the crowds at Memorial Stadium, University of Texas, Austin. I can remember as a child how left out I felt when I would hear that mighty roar drifting my way on a southern breeze, indicating a Texas score. But more often than not I was a voice in that roar, sitting in the knothole section and cheering the heroics of legends like Bohn Hilliard and Harrison Stafford. I've had the good fortune to know so many of those University athletic heros not only as performers and coaches but as people. Coach Clyde Littlefield had enough compassion for a freckle-faced kid to allow him to sack footballs for him after the practice had ended. D. X. Bible, Blair Cherry, Ed Price, Darrell Royal, Fred Akers have been personal bonuses to life in Austin. And include the All-American water boy, Rooster Andrews, and three-time All-American Hub Bechtol in that category.

I drove past Memorial Stadium the other day. A rare parking space opened up, and I took advantage of it to visit the site of so many memories. A gray mist was falling and the air was chilled, so I had the field to myself. It was not difficult to picture those stadium seats full of people. I could almost hear the cheers of thousands of voices, the strains of "Texas Fight," the sounds of foot meeting ball and body meeting body in violent collision.

It's incredible, the importance many of us place on the few occasions when football is played on those one hundred yards of fake grass: only five or six days a year. Legends are born and live forever in a matter of seconds. It required Jack Crane of Nocona, Texas, probably thirty seconds to run the football an incredible distance in all directions in covering the eighty or so yards to the goal line when Texas beat Arkansas in the fading moments of a game played on that field, I believe in 1939. Yet that short flash of time is as much a part of the stadium as the concrete and steel are, and it will be forever.

That green field was covered in ice on a cold November day in 1961. A late hit by a Texas Christian University lineman put Texas running sensation James Saxton out of the game and guaranteed a Horned Frog upset. It all happened in a twinkling of an eye, but the event still lives in the memories of avid Longhorn fans.

Earl Campbell played how many times in that arena? Nineteen or twenty? Around six hours of football. But in those few hours a lifetime of memories were created and a lucrative career was begun.

There are people, besides members of the coaching staff, who have arranged their entire lives just to be a part of those few hours of football played at Memorial Stadium each year. One of the most astute and talented businessmen I know, Bill Sansing, a former University of Texas Sports Information Director and now business partner and adviser to Jack Nicklaus, swears he has shaped his life so as to be a part of the Memorial Stadium community in his hometown of Austin.

Everywhere I travel I encounter Texas exes who have a common lament: "I wish I could live in Austin so I could be there for football season." When a position comes open on the University of Texas sports publicity staff, applications come from prominent lawyers, journalists, and business people who are willing to take the job just to be a part of the Memorial Stadium scene.

The rain began to fall harder, so I left my reverie and headed for the shelter underneath the stands. I swear I heard the strains of "The Eyes of Texas" playing in the background. Strange that the band would be practicing on such a rainy, cold day . . .

Cactus and the coach: Football legend Darrell Royal.

Darrell Royal

If it weren't for recruiting, Darrell Royal would still be one of the greatest coaches in the game of football. One of the true "generals" of the game sounded his own retreat from it because he had grown weary of the tactics being used by other coaches to grab off the blue chip athletes for their own schools. Anyone who doesn't think there are a lot of under-the-table shenanigans going on in that annual athlete roundup would bet on Slippery Rock against Notre Dame.

There's also a matter of dignity. There's nothing dignified about a coach sitting in a dingy motel in some small southern town day after day waiting for a chance to talk to some high school senior and his family. It's difficult for an honest coach to assume the manner of a door-to-door brush salesman, a role so often a part of the courtship ritual in trying to sign a player. And often that player is playing a game of cat-and-mouse, hiding from the coaches, in some cases even kidnapped by a coach to keep him from the others. It's a demeaning part of the coaching game. Darrell Royal grew tired of the charade and the dishonesty of other coaches.

Then, too, there was the press blitz that grew out of a tiff with University of Oklahoma coach Barry Switzer. Switzer had intimated that Darrell Royal had grown fat with success and was more intent on listening to the guitar picking of his many country music friends than getting out into the recruiting arena and mixing it up with the boys. (Incidentally, Coach Switzer is now promoting his own country music protege.)

There had been other controversies between the two, a reported Oklahoma spy casing the University of Texas practices and Royal challenging Switzer to a lie detector test. Challenge unaccepted. So when the day of Royal's last encounter with Oklahoma in that famed Cotton Bowl annual shootout arrived, the emotional pot was boiling. During the "wishbone T" years, I became a part of the Darrell Royal team as co-host of his television show. This took me to the games with the team. As chance would have it, I was talking to Darrell at midfield during the team warm-up exercises just before the kickoff of the University of Oklahoma game. Switzer came wandering up, impeccable in red slacks, white shirt, smile, and sculptured hair. His pearly teeth spread across his handsome face as he extended Darrell a diplomatic hand, which the Texas coach accepted. They exchanged a few pleasantries and then Switzer made his pitch. "You know, Darrell, the press really blew that 'guitar picking' remark out of proportion, didn't they?"

Darrell's famous jutted jaw thrust forward like the blade of a bulldozer. Looking the Oklahoma University coach straight in the eyes (as he does everyone he encounters), the former O.U. football great who had chosen Texas said, "No, they didn't. You were wrong, dead wrong in making that crack. You know full well that I am out there recruiting with everyone else. One of these days when you get a little further down the road, you'll realize how wrong you were."

Straight through the center of the line in a cloud of dust. Switzer's face turned redder than the O.U. grandstands, stammered a semi-answer, and suddenly found other duties to occupy him.

The script called for Royal and Texas to win that one. For many, the 6–6 tie was a moral victory for the 'Horns. But the disappointment in Darrell's locker-room face after the game told his inner feelings. And the fatigue so evident was a grim reminder of the toll of the game.

Football lost a legend when Darrell K. Royal hung 'em up after that season. He's still a young man who could compete with the best of them, but the game no longer deserves him. It's been turned over to the rich alums and the shady recruiters. And the final score is: THEM 7, FOOTBALL 0.

Fayetteville Shootout

There are costs in going to the summit. Once you have skinny-dipped with Bo Derek, swimming is never the same. I should never have been in that football stadium on that dreary December day, because never again will the game so touch me.

Fayetteville, Arkansas, December 6, 1969. The game of the century. It was football's one-hundredth anniversary and the premier game of that celebration. Texas, number one in the nation, was playing Arkansas, number two in the nation, not only for the Southwest Conference championship, but also for the national championship.

For a number of heady years, the "wishbone-T" years, I had the privilege of co-hosting "The Darrell Royal Television Show": fame through association. That meant attending many of the team practices, traveling with the squad, and getting up early on Sunday mornings to tape the show. They were giddy years, and they were also wearisome ones. It was a thrill to be caught up in the drama of some of those encounters, many of them in far-off places like Seattle, Boston, San Francisco, and Los Angeles. But far and above this game stands out in my memory, and in the memory of all football fans who watched those four historic quarters.

I shared a hotel suite with Darrell Royal in nearby Rogers, Arkansas, the night before the game. The rooms could have come without beds. No one in our suite touched theirs. Darrell had begun his sideline pacing in the hotel room hours before kickoff. All night long he was calling his coaches, suggesting possible game situations and discussing the proper response.

I'll never forget the grim silence of the team as they loaded into the buses that would carry us to the stadium.

Even talkative quarterback James Street was silent, a Street first. There was an atmosphere in that stadium that enveloped you like ether. The foggy, cold, drizzly air crackled with drama. The red Hogs of Arkansas were already hysterical hours before the kickoff. Razorback fans would drive miles and cheer the skinning of a pig to make a football cover. But with these stakes they reached a frenzy never before seen in that football-mad state. You knew that history was to be made that day. You knew it by the bristling of the hair on the back of your neck, by the chills that yo-yoed up and down your spine, by the pale silence of the players.

The entire nation was there, either quivering in the sea of red filling the stadium or perched in their easy chairs in front of the television. It would have seemed perfectly plausible if Red Grange, Jim Thorpe, and the Gip had returned for this one. Though President Nixon received a tremendous ovation when he helicoptered in, the Arkansas water boy got a bigger hand. God's number one football fan, Billy Graham, blessed the game, and the players immortalized it.

Ironically, as you all know, Texas won the game by a wild fourth down pass from James Street to Randy Peschal called by the man I had dubbed "the Barry Goldwater of collegiate football," Darrell Royal. The stunned silence of the Arkansas fans after the final pistol could be heard all the way to Little Rock.

Then a montage of memories, the unbridled hysteria in the Texas dressing room, President Nixon in the middle of them proclaiming the 'Horns number one in the nation, the hazardous bus ride through the insults of angered Razorbacks back to Ft. Smith to catch our plane, and then the wild celebration when we landed at the Austin airport, actually trapped inside the plane for thirty minutes by the 'Horn throngs who spilled out onto the runway. That was the game of a lifetime for those of us who were lucky enough to be there. But, after visiting the summit, football for many of us will never be the same.

Freddie Steinmark

When I first saw him on the plane that was flying the Texas football team back from California I thought he was one of the water boys. He was dwarfed by the baby beef herd of Longhorns. But later, when I saw Freddie Steinmark perform in the defensive backfield, he became seven feet tall. He would become even taller in the eyes of everyone who knew him.

The elation of the great Texas victory over Arkansas in the game of the century played in Fayetteville and the post-game locker room pronouncement by President Nixon that the Longhorns were number one in the nation was short-lived. Coach Royal was in New York City accepting the McCarthy Trophy, emblematic of the national collegiate football championship, when he received word that the leg injury that Freddie had played with had been diagnosed as cancer. He was to be operated on the next day at the Anderson Cancer Clinic in Houston. Darrell chartered a plane and flew to his bedside. The next day they removed Freddie's leg—bone cancer.

A few weeks later Freddie and I stood alone, except for a camera crew, in the middle of the field on which he and his teammates had received so much glory. There is no place lonelier than a deserted stadium. And on this day as a cold gray norther blew cruel winds across the fading yardline stripes, we stood shivering in the cold and in the truth of the moment. Both in the shadow of cancer, he but days after his operation, me just ten months after my own. We were making a film for the American Cancer Society.

Freddie spoke with candor of his battle. He was a fighter. A man his size who had succeeded in a game of giants was a proven battler. But now he was facing the fight of his life. He knew the odds. He knew they were poor. But odds were for gamblers. He was a performer.

When Texas played Notre Dame in the Cotton Bowl January 1, 1970, Freddie Steinmark was on the Texas sidelines, not on the bench, but pacing up and down the field on his crutches. Freddie played that game. He was in there every play. Not his hands, not his legs, but his spirit was out there intercepting Joe Theisman's passes, tackling runners who had eluded the linebackers. Freddie played that game and was a factor in the brilliant Longhorn victory over the Irish.

A few weeks later the Texas fans jammed Austin's Municipal Auditorium for the annual football banquet and celebration. As I called off the names of the players who had lettered, Coach Royal, with the Texas tradition, Rooster Andrews, assisting, was handing out the jackets and the awards.

You could feel the tension building as we ran down the list in alphabetical order. Finally I came to the S's. I called out the name Freddie Steinmark. My voice echoed through a silent auditorium. From the wings across the mammoth stage from us came a single small figure. Slowly, carefully, but *alone* walked Freddie Steinmark on his new artificial leg. It took an eternity and that walk will be remembered for an eternity. First the tears—in every eye. And then the cheers that rocked that auditorium like the eruption of 5000 personal volcanoes.

Freddie made it, like he said he would. He walked across the stage to receive his letter. For one evening, at least, he was the victor over cancer.

Davy Crockett's Revenge

It was the week Texas invaded Mexico twenty years ago. The Texas forces were led by Western Publications publisher, Joe Small. His mirthful band included CBS humorist John Henry Faulk; the dean of outdoor writers, Hart Stilwell; legendary photographer Russell Lee; the Huck Finn of architecture, animal-roping A. D. Stenger; and yours truly, a newly become television performer.

Joe Small had convinced the operators of Mexico's Trans Mar de Cortez Airlines that a junket of these semimad Texans to the newly completed resorts and splendid fishing waters of Baja California would result in an influx of visitors that would rival the California gold rush. So it was "su casa es mi casa"—that much Spanish we knew.

Troopmaster Small was good in freeloading but lousy in chemistry. The combination of urban John Henry Faulk down from New York City and outdoorsy and caustic Hart Stilwell was a social version of Montezuma's revenge. (John Henry in rebutting his high IQ grade remarked to Hart that fishing was for illiterates, egg suckers, and chicken pluckers. That's like telling Exxon that oil sucks. This began a running debate that endured for days.)

After surviving a kamikaze flight over the Sierra Madres in an ancient DC-3, we were treated to the favors of lovely and hospitable La Paz on the matchless Bay of La Paz. We knew we were among sane people when we saw coconut and palm trees standing in the center of buildings that had been built around them. We scuba dived, fished, toured, and became intimately acquainted with a new Mexican delicacy called the margarita. We should have stayed with Margarita. Instead, one morning we deserted her for orange soda water and tequila while being given a sight-

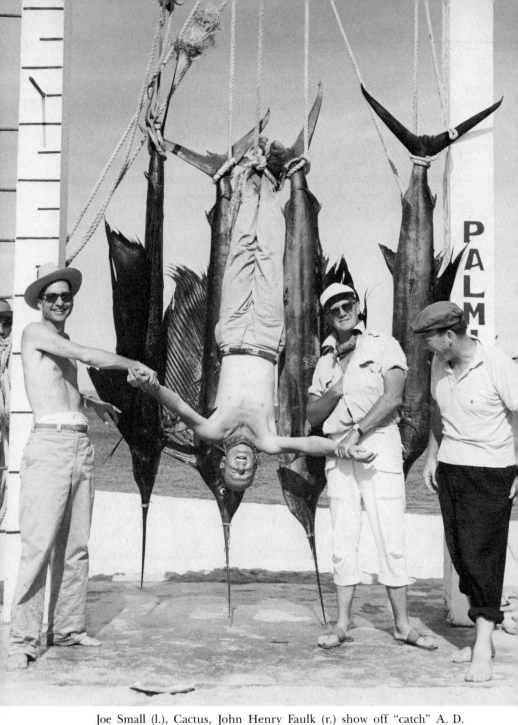

Joe Small (l.), Cactus, John Henry Faulk (r.) show off "catch" A. D. Stenger in Baja California.

seeing tour of La Paz in two ancient taxis. Orange soda water and José Cuervo give you strange urges—like the desire to drive to the tip of the Baja California peninsula one hundred and fifty miles away. We so instructed our two incredulous drivers.

"But *señors*," they rightfully protested, "there are only thirty miles of road between here and there."

All the more reason to go, we reasoned. So we filled up with Pemex and orange soda water and tequila and off we went—six crazy Texans in two crazy taxis driven by two fear-crazed drivers who had been given instructions to humor our wildest wish.

Sure enough, the semi-road lasted but thirty miles. It was replaced by dry creek beds, goat trails, and hunches. We drove into villages where the natives had never seen a car. The dogs didn't even know they were supposed to chase us. We bumped and rattled through deep desert canyons and over mountains. Occasionally we'd come upon some little pearl of a sandy beach rimming the Gulf of California, where we'd swim and sleep in hammocks as close to the stars as we'd ever been. Several days later we drove into the tiny fishing village of San José del Cabo at the very tip of Baja. Christopher Columbus received no such welcome, but then his journey was not so hazardous.

The next day we fished. The sailfish and marlin were right offshore where the waters of the Gulf and the Pacific merge in startlingly different hues. The huge billfish were actually asleep on the surface. We'd choose the one we wanted, troll our bait by him, and wham. Explosion. Skeptical John Henry became the world's greatest fishing devotee. Stilwell got his story. Lee and I got our photographs and our innocent Mexican hosts got a taste of the hazards of tourism.

The Texas Inland Navy

Luxurious yachts on Texas inland waters? Try that one on the folks in Minnesota and you can hear the eyebrows lifting all the way to Waxahachie. But there's a navy of large cruisers on Lake Texoma, the body of water that divides Texas and Oklahoma even more dramatically than does the Texas-Oklahoma University game.

My youngest son, Dayne, and I spent a recent weekend with Billy and Mary Williams of Dallas on their boat, which would have made Conrad Hilton wonder why there wasn't a strip of paper across the john and where they were hiding the Gideon Bibles and his autobiography. We had our choice of three air-conditioned bedrooms, each with its own private bathroom. We dined in a dining room that offered everything but a maitre d' and there was enough room on deck for the Budweiser team of Clydesdale horses. We settled for a case of their product.

You find these landlocked seagoing vessels more frequently moored snugly in their giant boathouses. They are lined up side by side like the mansions in an exclusive neighborhood. Highland Park on the water. Most of them have carpeted patios on the docks alongside their boat with lawn furniture and bars; all the outside comforts without crabgrass. Occasionally they venture out onto the huge lake formed by the dammed Red River and dwarf the smaller fishing and skiing boats. When the big boaters go fishing, they have their own smaller fishing boats.

We enjoyed luxuriating in our floating weekend home, but my son and I discovered an even greater pleasure when we experienced our first encounter with the striped bass that have been planted in the lake. It was a new fishing experience. Our guide, Cecil Price of nearby Sherman, seldom looked at the water as we cruised the lake. His eyes were glued to a fish-finding device that looks somewhat like one of those electronic games you can now play on your television set. Suddenly, his small screen would light up like the Astros' scoreboard on a good night. He'd stop the motor and instruct us to drop the huge silver spoons we were using to the bottom of the lake, 40 or 50 feet down. We would then reel in our lines as rapidly as possible. And almost always when the lights on the screen were dancing, we would be greeted with a strike that would register on the Richter scale.

My son, Dayne, hooked the first one. Ten minutes later he had brought to surface a creature that looked like something you'd wait for cold weather to butcher. Twenty-three pounds of striped bass, the sea bass that has flourished so in these north Texas inland waters. Thirteen times we brought these magnificent fighters to our landing net. The smallest weighed 12 pounds and the largest 28. It was one of those magical days when we were at the right place, at the right time, with the right wherewithal to make fishing memories that will stay with us all of our lives.

We learned something else about striped bass fishing in Texoma: Fishermen are like sea gulls. Haul in one fish and here come the boats. Dunkirk could have used such an armada. As soon as the boats arrived, the fish cut out for other feeding grounds. Our guide would then desert the fleet and use his magical machine to locate another school. We'd deplete the class by one or two before the Chinese navy arrived again to scatter the bass once more.

That evening we sat on the back of our friend's yacht dining on fried striped bass and watched the Dallas Cowboys beat the Houston Oilers on color television as the Texas sun sank slowly into the Oklahoma waters. Not a bad life, being a part of the Texas Inland Navy.

Cactus' favorite Lab, Ol' Yeller.

Ol' Yeller and ESP

Researchers have been conducting experiments to determine if dogs have extrasensory perception (ESP). They're wasting their time. I've already proven that they do.

My first Labrador retriever, Ol' Yeller, proved time after time that he could read my mind. He could not only read my thoughts, he changed them. When my friend, John Ramsey, presented me with a six-week-old ball of fur, he didn't realize what he was doing to us both. Because of that gift, John is now with me as co-owner and full-time manager of a boarding kennel, having forsaken a lucrative business in Dallas in order to go to the dogs in Austin. Not only did that puppy get me into the kennel business, it became the most driving force in my life for a period of ten years.

I should explain that Ol' Yeller was as black as the economic forecast. I had promised author Fred Gipson that I would name my next dog after his famous Old Yeller if he would name his next son Cactus. Since Fred was sixty-eight and single, he figured that was a good deal, I hadn't figured on owning a black dog.

Ol' Yeller and I took on retriever training and went out into the fields to learn a new sport. He taught me a lot, and apparently I didn't hinder him too much. No one had told us that you weren't supposed to teach a Lab to take hand signals until he was two years old. Therefore by the time Yeller was six months old, he was performing like a retriever much older.

We went to our first field trial, and when the judges got through laughing at me for my ridiculous efforts at handling a dog, they awarded us the second-place trophy. Ol' Yeller went on to win many field trials, including qualifying for four national championships, winning the title of Amateur Field Champion and Field Champion. He also captured a rare doubleheader by winning the Open and Amateur Stakes in the same trial—a feat comparable to a pitcher throwing two consecutive no-hitters.

We accomplished all this because Ol' Yeller has ESP. He knew hours before I began preparations that we were leaving for a field trial. He would take on his field trial look—tail wagging, that porpoise-like happy smile on his face, jumping up and down in anticipation of the birds he knew he would retrieve. He knew. At the trial, when the gunners downed three birds that all of the dogs were having difficulty finding, I would merely think of where I wanted Yeller to go. He would do so and find the birds that the other dogs couldn't find.

On a blind retrieve in field trials, the handler handles the dog with voice and hand commands to a hidden bird. Only the handler and the judges know the location of the bird. I remember one particularly tough blind that the judges had bragged would give all the dogs trouble. The dogs would take a straight line across the water in the direction toward the bird. An island full of briars in their pathway would divert their course, and the handlers would find it very difficult to get them back on the right track.

I talked it over with Yeller in my mind. "Yeller, now when you get to that island, swim around it to the left. Then come back around to the right again and resume your course." If he had come from IBM, he wouldn't have done a more perfect job. The judges were dumbfounded, but Ol' Yeller and I weren't surprised at all. After all, that's why the Lord gave dogs ESP.

Bolivor H. Tootwater

Just when you're beginning to think they are humans, dogs will do something to remind you that they are animals. You can tie a pink bow in the coiffured hair of your precious little poodle; you can put a brightly colored sweater on your boxer to help keep him warm; you can feed them dog food that's shaped like hamburger patties, put diamond chokers around their cute little necks, and hug 'em and even kiss them. You can shower them with all those anthropomorphic things, but you'll still have a dog on your hands.

Bolivor H. Tootwater, our loyal, courageous basset hound, is living proof of this fact. We've given Bolivor a distinguished name befitting one of high rank. We have showered him with his own condominium and an engraved, silver-coated food dish. He's had his long, digging nails manicured; he has even had his flowing, regal ears shampooed. So how does he show his appreciation for these acts of love? Well, take last week for example—the day the snows came. Knowing how Bolivor enjoys frolicking in snow and taking walks in the woods, I donned my heavy boots and jacket, and we headed down the trail leading through the cedar thickets.

"Bolivor," I said, and I do talk to my very intelligent companion, "this is a rare moment. It's not often that we have snow here in central Texas, as you well know, Bolivor. So I'm glad that you and I have the good sense to be out here in the woods to enjoy the beauty and rarity of this moment."

Bolivor wagged his tail in total agreement.

"Yessir, old friend," I continued, "there's something almost sacred in being out in the beauty of God's world with a true and understanding friend. And that's what I consider you to be. We are not master and servant. We are true *amigos*. And I want you to know that I appreciate you, Bolivor. I appreciate the fact that you never question any of my decisions, unless they involve you and water. I'm grateful that you never complain and never ask for a thing until near feeding time. It is also reassuring to know that you are always near; that no matter how lonely I may be, I need but call your name and you are at my side."

The snow was falling harder and a soft white meringue was covering the earth, making rocky places look soft and decorating the cedar trees with the look of Christmas. Bolivor's long, robe-like ears were making twin trails in the snow as he trotted to my side.

Suddenly, I literally reeled back as if shot. My nostrils were filled with an odor that would have gagged Bigfoot. Where was it coming from? Not Bolivor, he was twenty feet away from me and upwind. Then he heeled to my side. My nostrils were aflame as if inhaling acid. It was Bolivor. The primitive animal instincts had taken over when my companion had come upon the remains of a very dead deer. In the ancient ways of his breed, he had rolled in the rotten carcass. Legend says this is how an animal being pursued covers its scent.

Our brotherhood was broken. Bolivor was ordered to a distance far behind me. And days after our walk in the snow, he was still not recovered from the trauma of his hour-long shampooing. And he is once again regarded as a basset hound DOG.

The Incredulous Bear

Having A. D. Stenger and me as neighbors, the doctor thought he was ready for almost anything. But when we came to his front door and said, "Doc, we have a guy here who was bitten by a bear in the canyon down there behind your house," we perturbed the imperturbable. It's not the usual case a doctor living in a highly developed Austin suburban area receives.

It was all part of A. D. Stenger's roping mania. Not only was he not content after having gone almost to the North Pole to rope a polar bear, now he wanted films of a man almost in his seventies roping a bear. When he approached me with his idea of producing an action sequence for television of former game warden, guide, hunter, and wild critter roper Bob Snow in which he would rope a huge brown bear, I considered a rope for A. D.— with thirteen loops in it. Foolishly I went along with the scheme more in unbelieving fascination than in sound judgment. Sound judgment was never a factor in any of A. D.'s escapades. I even recruited friends and relatives to assist in the filming—John Henry Faulk, who was old enough to know better, and my brother Wally, who was young enough to need the lesson.

Stenger had obtained a bear for the film by buying one from a carnival that no longer wanted the trained creature because it had decided to invent some tricks of its own— like attacking its handler. In the bottom of a deep canyon practically within the sound of the voices of the lobbyists in our state capitol building, A. D. had constructed a camera platform on wheels situated on a track so that it had lateral movement. From this vantage point Stenger was to do his filming. Brother Wally was stationed on top of a cliff to get the wide shots. John Henry's job was to hold a microphone attached to a long pole over the action to capture the sound. My assignment was to push the camera platform on which Stenger was situated.

The entire area for the film had been fenced in by Stenger and his faithful work crew of one, Phillip, who had the remarkable facility of being able to accept any task that his employer assigned him without question. The script called for the bear to be released from its cage, at which point a pack of hound dogs were to be released also. The bear would be encouraged to proceed down the canyon toward the cameras, and the hounds would follow and corner the bear. At this point veteran Bob Snow would enter the scene, rope the bear, tie it to a tree, and the adventure epic would be complete. So went the battle plan. However, Stenger neglected to inform the bear.

Things went well until Snow made his entrance and roped the animal. Then there was considerable ad-libbing. Snow quickly made a hitch with the rope around a tree. Duck soup for a trained carnival bear. He merely reversed directions and quickly unhitched the hitch, dispensing dogs in all directions at the same time, and next I saw of Bob Snow's right thigh, it was disappearing into the mouth of a very testy brown bear.

Enter Bob Snow Junior into the arena with a tear gas pistol in hand. He fired just as the actors shifted positions. The pellet landed near Bob Snow Senior's head, sending him into convulsions of coughing as if he didn't have enough problems already. Drama be damned, I decided, as I took a huge stick and applied it to the bear's nose, which he now decided to take elsewhere.

Bob Snow's thigh survived, due to the absence of many teeth in the ancient animal's sugar-spoiled mouth. But the doctor said it was the worst case of bear gumming that he'd ever treated.

As to the film? There were technical difficulties. In the heat of the action, our cameraman had forgotten to turn the cameras on. That's show biz.

Heavenly Dogs

Dear Son:

I've been thinking about the question you asked me yesterday afternoon when we were down by the lake throwing sticks into the water for Old Blackie to retrieve. You remember you asked me if dogs go to heaven? I didn't take the time to answer then, because about that time those bluejays decided to buzz Old Blackie and he took out after them and we had to call him back.

Well, son, the answer to your question is: Of course, dogs go to heaven. How could it be heaven without them? Heaven is where everything is perfect and how could it be perfect without a dog to fetch the stick that you throw in the water or to meet you with a smile on his face and a wag on his tail when you come in from choir practice? Can you imagine a heaven without a dog to wrassle with in clover greener and softer than any you've ever seen? And can you picture the fun it must be to watch a good pointer coming to point when he senses a flock of angels behind a cloud? Or playing catch with a high jumper, using your halo as a Frisbee? Can you imagine there not being a place in heaven for seeing eye dogs, who spend their whole lives serving their masters? Why, in heaven they can walk by their masters' sides without a harness, and there's never a stoplight to worry about. In fact there's no traffic at all, and dog and master can see one another and not worry about a single thing.

And you know what, son? Heaven is full of cats that just love to be chased by dogs. And there's a tree always within easy reach, not that they need it for safety, but dogs just love to chase cats and cats just love to climb trees to get away from them. And the dogs appreciate the trees, too. Can you imagine, son, a heaven without a dog to play with in the cloud drifts? They're just like the snowdrifts that you and Old Blackie frolic in, except they're not cold and they're much softer.

And if there were no dogs in heaven, who would the angels talk to when they wanted to get off by themselves and confide in someone who would never reveal what he was told? And son, would you believe that there's a St. Bernard on every corner in heaven, with a keg of fruit juice free for the taking? And every day there are greyhound races with uncatchable rabbits. And there are sheepdogs to round up the stray clouds and basset hounds and beagles to make a joyful noise unto the Lord.

And how could it be heaven without a dog to curl up in front of the fire and give a low grunt of pure satisfaction when you lie down with him and put your arm around him? And of course there has to be a dog to wake you up every morning by jumping on your bed and licking you in your face and saying, "Come on, let's go have a heavenly time."

And son, you just know that sittin' at the feet of God as He runs things from His heavenly home there's a God-like dog, because son, you see, we're made in the image of God and God made us always to be with a dog. So to answer your question: Yes, son, dogs *do* go to heaven.

Only at Cisco's

The well-dressed couple asked for a table for two. The waiter led them through a throng of laughing, drinking, eating people and prepared to seat them at a table for four that was occupied by two other people.

"We don't want to sit with anyone else. We want to sit by ourselves," said the man.

"Well, if you don't like this table, gawd damn it, you can go to Luby's," barked the waiter.

Only at Cisco's Bakery in Austin. They offer the best *migas* and the most irreverent waiters in America. And the irreverence of the waiters is not extended only to the customers—owner and proprietor Rudy Cisneros gets the same treatment.

The late "Moscow" was legendary as a waiter. Rudy fired him weekly for one reason or another three or four. One morning, after having fired Moscow the evening before, Rudy called his place of business and was surprised to hear the fired waiter answer the phone with "Cisco's. Manager speaking."

"Moscow," blurted Rudy, "what are you doing there?"

"Workin'," replied Moscow and promptly hung up the phone.

Although Cisco's is visited by people from all walks of life, and is the most integrated restaurant in Texas, everyone receives equal treatment. Governor Preston Smith once gave Moscow the political gladhand treatment.

"Hi, Moscow," said the guv.

"Hi," replied Moscow. "Who are you?" And he wasn't kidding.

Rudy started his uniquely Austin establishment twenty-eight years ago as a bakery, which it remains. But for the last twenty years or so it's the cafe that packs them in. You'll see Brown Berets sitting next to the likes of Governor Clements, ditch diggers enjoying their food alongside

"Mr. Proprietor" Rudy Cisneros (holding cigar) and the gang at Cisco's Bakery. (Photograph by Don Pryor.)

John Connally. Darrell Royal is a Cisco's regular, and he introduced Willie Nelson and many other country music star regulars to Rudy's delicious *migas* (scrambled eggs with corn tortilla chips, fresh tomatoes, onions, cheese, special sauce, and sausage), enchiladas, fajitas, and other house specialties.

There has been a poker game or two played in the rear room of Cisco's after hours. And, a few years back, it was rumored that you could get from Rudy the betting line on a football game in order to place a wager.

A voice on Rudy's phone one morning said, "Rudy, what's the line this morning?"

Replied the straight-talking proprietor, "You s.o.b. I don't give the line on the games until eleven o'clock."

"Rudy," the caller said, "this is Darrell Royal. And I only wanted to know how long the waiting line is. I've got some friends in town and we're hungry."

And the line is always long at Cisco's on the mornings after a Texas home football game. Breakfast at Cisco's is as traditional as the orange tower.

What you get for breakfast is according to the mood of your waiter. I remember the time I asked Darrell Cluck, Rudy's "token gringo" waiter, for two eggs over easy.

"We don't have time to fry eggs," barked Rudy's minority member. "You'll get *migas*."

I did.

Trying to reach Rudy by telephone is an adventure. Once Waggoner Carr, a Cisco's regular, called for Rudy but jokingly asked Moscow for the proprietor. The deadly serious waiter walked into the dining room and shouted, "Is there a Mr. Proprietor here?" He returned to the phone and said, "There ain't no Mr. Proprietor here." And hung up.

The area of east Austin where Cisco's is located is no stranger to emergency ambulance and police calls. But in twenty-eight years, Rudy's place has never once been burglarized. Rudy attributes this to the fact that he has a friendly word for everyone he encounters—even if his waiters don't.

An Austin tradition—"Dirty Martin's" Kum-Bak Place. (Photograph by Don Pryor.)

Dirty Martin's

Take back your clowns. Use those huge arches for giant croquet games. Not for me the pre-prepared, the self-prepared, the formula-prepared. I'll get my hamburgers at Dirty Martin's, if you please.

It's not that theirs are the only hamburgers. Hamburgers are like barbecue; about the only way they come is good. But Dirty Martin's burgers come with a special ingredient—tradition.

Since 1926, the little frame two-story building on the University drag on Guadalupe has been serving the same basic product. There's hardly a living University of Texas student or ex-student who hasn't dined on these heavenly hamburgers. There are thousands of us who practically majored in Dirty Martin's while attending the University in that we spent more time there than in the classroom or library. I learned sociology while socializing with friends at the most popular drive-in in town. I might have flunked history at U.T., but I passed current events at Dirty's.

And I've learned quite a bit about philosophy from Doc, who has been hopping cars at Martin's Kum-Bak, as it is officially named, since way back in 1954. Doc always has time to visit after he brings the tray of burgers to your car, and many a University or high school student has benefited from this kindly man's affection and concern. Doc's partner Andy was a part of the Dirty Martin's tradition until he departed in 1973 for the big hamburger drive-in in the sky, where the tips are big and the customers patient. The inside help remains about the same over the years. The same big hands shaping the meat into patties with tender loving care that no machine could duplicate. Even turning them over without a spatula. The same waitress knowing what beer to put in front of what customer without even bothering to take the order. And the same ancient grills making their same magic as they have consistently done over the years. They're only getting better with age, not only cooking but seasoning the meat with the flavor that comes from time and use.

Dirty Martin's is not dirty, actually. To my knowledge, they've always passed the necessary health inspection codes. But somewhere along the way, Dirty Martin's, like "hook-'em-horns" and "the forty acres," became permanent jargon in Austin, Texas, language.

Martin's Kum-Bak is an appropriate name, though, because you always come back to Dirty's. You'll see, as you drive by, gray and balding heads among the coiffured locks of the new Martin's generations. For only at this hamburger joint do the products contain a burnt orange flavor. And the older you are, the better the burger, because at my age you don't have to cut the onions in anticipation of the socialization that used to follow on Mt. Bonnell or at Zilker Park.

Chili Silly

I have never been to a chili cook-off. I may lose my Texan citizenship with this admission. I have been invited to judge dozens of them. As a broadcaster I have interviewed scores and scores of participants or promoters of these festivals of masochism. But I refuse to be lured into attending. In the first place, a chili cook-off in Texas in the summer makes as much sense as a water festival in the Sahara. Yet many of the contests are staged in the very season when those with saner tastes are involved with ice cream, watermelon, and lemonade. In the second place, I have read the recipes used by some of these stomach assassins. If I choose suicide as an exit, I will choose a more painless means.

I will admit that some of those who participate in these culinary shenanigans are friends of mine. I embrace all of mankind but with certain reservations. The late Wick Fowler of Austin and Frank Tolbert of Dallas, who were the instigators of the chili cook-off held annually in Terlingua, I've known as friends. I think kindly of Gordon Fowler, Wick's son who's carrying on the family chili tradition with his 2-Alarm Chili product. Gordon is humane enough to allow the preparer the prerogative of naming his own degree of masochism as far as the heat of the chili is concerned by adding or excluding certain ingredients included in their package.

The main reason I do not attend chili cook-offs is that it would be senseless since I possess the greatest chili recipe in the world—mine. When you've feasted your eyes on Rembrandt, would you choose the work of a novice? When you've listened to Mozart, would you prefer the works of Hank Snow? When you've been to Rome, would you opt for Norman, Oklahoma? Of course not. So why should I be concerned with lesser chili?

I can't, of course, reveal the secrets of my chili. No true artist surrenders his special genius. However, I can tell you that my chili recipe has evolved over the years by borrowing from some of the great figures of Texas history. When Davy Crockett lay dying in the Alamo, he whispered one word to one of his Mexican executioners. That word was the name of one of the ingredients in my chili. Sam Houston, who lived with the Indians for many years, learned much from them. But the greatest gift he received from them was one of the more important ingredients in my chili. Indian legend has it that ill fortune will come to one who inherited that ingredient, as did I, if he reveals that secret.

Howard Hughes left another will that no one has been aware of until now. I was the beneficiary of Howard Hughes' personal secret chili ingredient. And California shall not have it! Texas Speaker Billy Clayton gave me yet another special ingredient that he had kept locked in his office desk drawer in the state Capitol for ten years. The special coloring agent in my chili was endowed to me by the great Texas artist, Porfirio Salinas—something he found growing in a bluebonnet patch.

So you can see, my chili is truly a historical, Texas mixture. Visit your chili cook-offs if you like. I judge not your childish proclivities. But when you want a real bowl of Texas chili, come see me. Chili mecca is not in Terlingua— it is within the shadow of the Capitol building of the state of Texas.

Brisketville, Texas

Ask the average Texan why he lives in Texas despite the searing summer heat, the monotony of western plains that stretch from here to yonder and back to here, the rattlesnakes and scorpions and pusillanimous vinegarroons and chances are he'll say "because of the barbecue."

You take the barbecue away from a Texan and you take away manna and heaven. It's said that a man on death row in Texas when asked his choice of fare for his last meal replied, "Warden, I want a barbecue dinner, of course. But cut the onions, they give me indigestion sumpthin' awful."

It's common knowledge among the clergy that God invented beef briskets for Texans and made the oak and mesquite trees to provide the heat and smoke for barbecuing them. He also established Elgin, Texas, so Elgin sausage could come from there and be barbecued and folded between a single slice of white bread to make the juiciest and most delightful delicacy to grace mankind.

Texans love barbecue. I can show you one stretch of U.S. 183 west of Austin where you could hit a three-wood 25 straight times and your ball would land on a different barbecue place everytime.

Aggies, T-sips, Republicans, Methodists, Catholics, Democrats, and even Baptists—the total Texas populace is in accord in the brotherhood of barbecue worship. However, there are rival factions. The sauce-cooked-on-the-meat folks versus the sauce-on-the-side folks (or no sauce at all). A popular barbecue restaurant chain in west Texas that featured barbecue marinated in their special sauce came to Austin and drowned in their own marinade. Austinites, they learned, prefer their barbecue sans sauce or like to add it at their discretion.

In my opinion barbecue is at its very best served on butcher paper, cut with a knife chained to the table, and eaten only with crackers, onions, and pickles in the same market where it was barbecued. Lockhart, Texas, will forever live in the hearts of Texans for so serving. Likewise Elgin and Giddings.

The purist barbecue connoisseur will tell you that slicing a brisket with an electric knife robs the meat of its special flavor. Electricity has no place in Texas barbecuing. And that goes for those grocery store electric rotisseries that defame the name of authentic Texas barbecue.

Some of the world's best barbecue is prepared on open pits, recently dug and filled with glowing coals, covered in chicken wire holding beef or chicken and sopped with mops covered in sauce. Chickens will volunteer to end their days in such delectable fashion. And the Lord gave us nostrils for the main purpose of filling them with the incredible aroma of the feast in the making, hour after tantalizing hour.

Texas has had many barbecue kings. The late Dale Baker of Austin was one of the most colorful and prolific. He would barbecue a rumor. Dale kept a jackass grazing on the grass adjacent to his cafe. One day it wasn't there. I asked of its whereabouts.

"Don't ask questions," was his reply, "and eat up."

The County Line of Austin is one of the current Texas leaders. The rustic Salt Lick near Driftwood, Texas, is barbecue eating in the delicious rough, and the famed Coupland Inn in Coupland, Texas, is the king of family-style serving.

But the man who catered the world with Texas barbecue was the late Walter Jetton of Fort Worth. His famous LBJ barbecues at the Pedernales White House did more for diplomacy than all the summit meetings put together, according to then Secretary of State Dean Rusk. Probably correct. Because, come to think of it, when did you last see a man frowning with a barbecued rib in his hand?

"La Cuenta por mi Amigo"

It was probably one of the dirtiest tricks played on the Allies during World War II. She was one of the "bundles from Britain." Her name was Barbara Bray and her parents had shipped her and her brother over from their London home to live with an aunt in Texas and avoid the German air blitzes. She would have been safer in England than exposed to my devious deeds. She had never sampled Texas Mexican food, so on our first date I took her to one of Austin's incomparable Mexican restaurants. She was eighteen and trusting, and I was eighteen and mean as hell. When she asked me what the bowl filled with chili sauce on the table was, I told her it was Mexican soup. She ate one spoonful of it, and there went the traditionally good American-British relationship.

Never mind. Mexican food has done more to cement positive relations between Austin and people from all over the world than almost any other factor. I wouldn't give you a taco shell for a Mexican restaurant that didn't start out as a mamacita and papacito operation in a little wooden house recently repainted in white with red and green trim. And if there isn't a bullfight on velvet oil painting on the wall, then beware—you're not getting authentic non-authentic Mexican food. Texas Mexican food is not authentic at all, of course. Once they discover it, Mexicans will come all the way from the Yucatán Peninsula to enjoy it. You can't get it there.

Where else but Austin would Mexican food be served to the members of the press covering a football game? I suspect this bonus has attracted more of the nation's press to the University of Texas press box than the football games being played below.

Matt Martinez of Austin is typical of the Tex-Mex Mexican food operators. He began in the little house after tiring of trying to make it as a newspaper boy and boxer. His El Rancho cafe, situated at the edge of downtown Austin, was where a legend was born. Matt has served more Texas politicians than a summons server. On any given day in that old house you could see the likes of Ben Barnes, Preston Smith, Price Daniel, Allan Shivers, Lyndon Johnson, J. Frank Dobie, Walter Prescott Webb, and just a bunch of people who didn't know these aforementioned celebs or particularly care.

Now El Rancho is situated across the street from where that old house stood before surrendering to asphalt and occupies two handsome Spanish-style buildings. The menu has grown too as in most Tex-Mex restaurants. Matt is an innovator. From the basic bowl of red and corn-wrapped tamales he has grown to more exotic dishes, including *chili relleno, tostadas compuestas con carne*, shrimp enchiladas, Mexican pizza, and all the other calorie counters' nightmares. I think the Texas legislature voted wet just so they could add margaritas to their dinners at El Rancho.

Like many other Mexican food operators, Matt is in the tortilla-manufacturing business and mechanization has replaced two skilled and patient hands in turning out those little round goodies.

You'll get an argument from some folks that the University of Texas or the state Capitol or the purple hills are Austin's greatest assets. Thousands believe the puffy taco is our greatest gift to the world. It's a toss-up, in my opinion.

In writing this essay, I was prompted to call Barbara Bray, now married to Dr. Michael Sachs in New York City. I read her the first paragraph. She corrected her age by two years and informed me that she might consider another go at Mexican food once she has recovered from her first encounter in 1942.

The Reality of Venison

I've encountered one person in my lifetime who did not have a special recipe for removing the wild taste from venison. He was a vegetarian from Tibet who did not know what meat was.

Next to how the Dallas Cowboys did last weekend, preparing venison is the favorite topic of Texas conversation. I am not a fancier of deer meat. I know, that makes me a commie suspect. But what can you expect from one who has never seen a professional football or baseball game in or out of the Astrodome?

The problem I find with deer meat is the same I find with fish. It doesn't taste like beef. My friends have tried to salvage me with venison taste-disguising recipes. Let me share a few.

Ira Hildebrand of Tyler and Pearsall, Texas, gave me this one: Soak the venison in yak's milk for twenty-four hours. Slice meat into very thin slices and press with a hot iron. Then marinate meat in a solution of Pearl beer, 2-Alarm chili, one-half pint of Gulf oil, a fifth of Brazos River water obtained and blessed in Waco, Texas, by Grant Teaff, and a margarita on the rocks from Matt Martinez's El Rancho restaurant in Austin. Let marinate for four days with Lawrence Welk records playing constantly in the background for tenderness. Chicken-fry and serve only between 11:00 p.m. and midnight. Guaranteed to remove the wild taste said Mr. Hildebrand. Still tastes like raw Whitetail says Mr. Pryor.

Texas outdoor writer George Bolton gave me this recipe: Clean deer immediately upon slaying and wrap carcass in raw silk soaked in olive oil (the guys in the hunting camp wondered why I brought these items along in my knapsack). Butcher deer under water (the lifeguard at Barton Springs was a handicap). Tenderize meat by pounding with a nine-iron, a lesser iron won't do the job. Massage meat for two hours with aloe vera lotion—also very good for your hands. Season with salt, black pepper, cayenne pepper, bay leaves, cloves, nutmeg, garlic, thyme, Worcestershire sauce, asphalt, A-1 sauce, hot sauce, Lilacs de France toilet water, sugar, sugar substitute, lemon juice, lime juice, papaya juice, horseapple juice, lye, and a dab of Copenhagen. Barbecue for twenty-four hours using Lithuanian dogwood for firewood. Serve on copper plates. Guaranteed to remove venison's wild taste said Mr. Bolton. Tastes like musky goat says Mr. Pryor.

Houston attorney Mike McCrory gave me his special recipe: Select only five point buck. Discard all but backstrap and cut meat into five steaks. Wrap steaks in bacon and bury in red clay for five days. Place meat in five plastic bags half filled with onions and garlic. Place bags in hot sun for five hours. Remove meat and soak for five minutes in five different wines. Freeze meat for five months. On the fifth day of the fifth month—May 5th—broil meat for five hours and five minutes. Will serve five people and guaranteed to remove wild taste of venison said Mr. McCrory. Tastes five ways like dead deer says Mr. Pryor.

Frustrated, I devised my own recipe. Proceed to deer lease. Climb into shooting blind. Shoot first steer that wanders by. Skin steer and attach antlers stolen from hunting camp wall. Butcher steer and prepare beef any way preferred. *Guaranteed* to remove wild venison taste.

Hoffman's Grocery

Gradually grocery stores have evolved into do-it-your-selfers. Now they have them where you even sack your own groceries. Recently, as I staggered to my car under the load of three sacks of hysterically expensive foodstuffs, my mind sought escape in memories of another day of grocery shopping.

In my mind's eye I went back to Mr. Hoffman's grocery at 40th and Speedway. I remembered how Grandmother would pick up the telephone when she needed something for supper and order it from Mr. Hoffman. In an hour or so here would come Otis, the grocery boy, in his Ford. Soon he would be knocking at the back door with a sack of groceries in hand. He never asked for cash. It was always "charge it."

Often as not, his delivery would include another item that Grandma had not ordered. Just something that Mr. Hoffman thought she would enjoy, like some fresh roastin' ears or a package of Beechnut Tobacco smuggled in, wrapped like candy to disguise the contents. Only Mr. Hoffman, Grandma, and I were in on Grandma's secret vice—a taste for Beechnut Chewing Tobacco. Often I was sent on a clandestine mission to Hoffman's grocery to procure one of these mysterious packages. I never resorted to blackmail, but then Grandma allowed for this temptation by tipping generously in candy from Hoffman's fascinating candy case, which was loaded with such goodies as chocolate soldiers, tootsie rolls, and licorice babies.

I'm sure the selection at Hoffman's Grocery was pitifully small compared to today's supermarkets. But at that time in life, it was the most spectacular accumulation of food and household items in the world. And what made it more fascinating was that much of it was displayed unwrapped in glass bowls for easy viewing. There was always the wonderful aroma of coffee beans being ground for a customer. And always the exhilarating prospect of selecting a Nehi soda water from the red soda water box full of all kinds of flavors cooled by cakes of ice. The procuring of one of these bottles of pop was a major motivation in my young life, a desire that led to all sorts of extraordinary deeds.

But my fondest memories of Hoffman's grocery are of Mr. and Mrs. Hoffman and the delivery boy, Otis. They were friends. They not only wanted your business, they wanted your company. They treated a barefoot, freckle-faced little feller like he was someone important. And everyone who came in their store *was* important to them.

Just for old time's sake, and for fun, I called the local supermarket the other day and asked for the manager. The first reaction was, "What is your complaint?" No complaint, I explained. I just wondered if they would please deliver a case of Nehi orange soda water, a dozen ears of corn, and a package of Beechnut Chewing Tobacco to my home. He hung up on me.

My Black-eyed Beauties

I can't remember when this love affair began. Perhaps it was the first time I looked into Hedy Lamarr's eyes. I was sitting in the front row of the theater, and she was on the silver screen. I was mesmerized by her eyes. I was an "eyes man" in those young days.

The next time I looked into those eyes they were swimming in their natural juices and cozying up to hunks of backstrap. And even today, all these years later, I think of Hedy Lamarr every time I eat black-eyed peas. The tragedy of the aging process is that now I'm a lot more interested in the peas than I am in the lady—and still would be if she looked now like she did then.

I am a black-eyed peaholic. If I couldn't eat them, I would sniff them. I found in the woman I married the traits that I had searched the world over for: She had eyes that looked like black-eyed peas, and she could, and can, cook black-eyed peas even better than my mother.

I am told that Yankees feed black-eyed peas to their cattle. With a mentality like that I cannot understand how the South managed to lose the Civil War to them. I suppose under some circumstance I too could feed black-eyed peas to a cow, but I'd sure have to love that cow.

Some people have a weird fascination with the food chosen by a condemned man for his last meal. Others think it's weirder to have an appetite for a last meal. But I can understand why one would want to conclude his days here on earth with his favorite food. Without a doubt, my choice, perish the thought, would be black-eyed peas, hot homemade cornbread with country fresh butter practically drowning it, and some barbecued pork ribs just to express my disdain for vegetarianism. (If the Lord hadn't meant for us to eat meat, He wouldn't have made tooth-picks.) And I would have an appetite, because I would have the joyous anticipation of a one-way trip to heaven, where all black-eyed peas are garden-fresh and where angels daily churn fresh butter while their mothers spend time lovingly preparing acres of cornbread.

Forever, poets have sung the praises of spring, for its gift of rebirth, for the return of birds and grass and flowers and the disappearance of snow and ice. They extol it as a time of union between man and woman, the season for romance. But I look upon spring as that magical season when you plant that tiny little black-eyed pea seed into the earth. And water it. And fertilize it. And wait for God to send forth his greatest miracle when that little seed pushes that first green harbinger of ecstasy through the ground.

When I see it, bells ring and birds sing, and the whole world is filled with a symphony of joy. Hallelujah, hallelujah, give praise to the coming of the black-eyed pea. We know they are here when the star shines bright over Athens, Texas, the Bethlehem of black-eyed peas, and the wise men come to pay homage to the annual birth of the tiny vegetable, and we celebrate and feast ourselves and give thanks that we live in a free land where we can eat all the black-eyed peas we want. God bless America and the black-eyed pea!

John Henry Faulk

I'm not above electronic poaching. So when I discovered that John Henry Faulk's CBS radio program from New York was being fed down the network line to Austin simply as a line test (it was not available to Texas) at the same time my own show was on the air, I borrowed bits of John Henry. I still borrow bits of John Henry Faulk anytime I need a good laugh line.

The native Austinite hit New York like a blue Texas norther—his presence was soon known by all. The war had just ended and the nation was ready for laughter. John Henry provided it with his Texas drawl and his Phi Beta Kappa wit. It was as if Mark Twain's mind had been put into Will Rogers' head. The sophisticated, penetrating insight of Twain expressed with the casual drawl and fun of Rogers. Suddenly John Henry Faulk was New York's darling.

His mother, then elderly and in poor health, longed to hear her son's radio programs here in Austin. But CBS was sharing him only with the eastern portion of the nation at the time. At least so they thought. I was my own controls operator during my afternoon show. I have never been a mechanically deft person and almost every afternoon I would demonstrate that truth by accidentally pushing the wrong button and John Henry's voice would fill the Austin airwaves. Mrs. Faulk and the sizable Austin Faulk clan were elated with my technical incompetence. My boss and the telephone company did not share their enthusiasm. But try as I would, I just couldn't seem to overcome my clumsiness. So John Henry became almost a regular feature on my show.

The first time he visited home the protege of J. Frank Dobie came to the studio and introduced himself to me. It

Cactus with longtime friend John Henry Faulk. (Photograph by Charles Guerrero.)

was one of the most significant introductions of my life. I've learned a lot from John Henry—such as that the world doesn't end at the Red River. He introduced me to New York City. He also introduced me to east Austin and made me realize that I had been living in a world that was almost totally white. Through John Henry I was given the priceless opportunity to sit at the feet of the Texas triumvirate—J. Frank Dobie, Walter Prescott Webb, and Roy Bedichek—and to feed on the wisdom of those legendary minds.

I learned a lot about courage from John Henry. I was in New York as his guest when the tentacles of McCarthyism reached out and almost strangled him. I watched in disbelief as his career was cut off as surely and cruelly as an executioner severs the head of the condemned. For six long years I saw him reel from blow after blow as innuendo and smear attacked him. But I never saw him down. He never lost his faith in the American system during those blacklisting years. And he never became bitter, even when having to accept food from friends to sustain him and his family. And when he won his lawsuit against his attackers and helped put an end to vigilantism in America, our faith in the American system of justice was sustained.

John Henry is back in Austin now with his wife, Liz, and his son, Yohan, and their twelve geese, forty chickens, and countless quail. His voice is still heard occasionally on my radio show. But now we have a controls operator. Uptown!

In the studio with sexy-voiced Jack Wallace.

Jack Wallace

His voice sounded like a gravel truck coasting through molasses. Women found it sexy. The voice of one who had been around but still had enough softness in him to be romantic. They would hear what had become the best known bedside voice in central Texas flowing out of their radios during the wee hours and would conjure up an image far different from the body that held Jack Wallace.

We found him in Brownwood, Texas, while searching for radio announcers. We were amazed to find that good a voice in that small a community. But we soon learned that predicting Jack Wallace was like finding an obscure address in San Antonio without a road map.

Back to Jack's sexy voice and the women. They would call him up in the middle of their lonely nights and tell him their troubles. Robert Young had never been so understanding and caring. Some women were unable to restrain themselves and would come to the studio desperate to meet this dreamy man. What they saw was a man in a pair of khaki shorts, beard down to his very round stomach usually unencumbered by a shirt, and hair draping his shoulders. A man carrying nearly three hundred pounds on five feet nine inches.

Jack was funny enough to be governor of Texas. People clamored to be in his company because he was sure laughter. He turned on easier than a television set in a motel room. For a number of years I could hardly wait to get to work—I so enjoyed doing a two-man radio show with him. We never rehearsed a line we said—never even discussed it. I would merely challenge his inventiveness and he never failed to come through. I would introduce him as a talking field of bluebonnets and that he would become, or a gay weathercaster or an ancient old maid. He was brilliant.

Television's Uncle Jay needed a sidekick. So we gave Jack the name of Packer Jack, put a beard and forty-niner clothes on him, and he became the idol of the kids. Uncle Jay was the right way; Jack was the wrong. He would send mothers into a tizzy by telling their little darlings not to worry about bathing—germs were healthy. But the kids knew what their mothers didn't—that Packer Jack was a clown and you're never supposed to take clowns seriously.

Jack was about half redneck and two-thirds Archie Bunker. But the hippies of the sixties would see his long hair and beard and consider him one of them—especially when Jack would be strolling down a street holding hands with his Gibbon's ape that looked like a son. They would yell at Jack and give him the two-finger V sign and he would return the greeting—minus one finger.

Jack Wallace stories are legend. The day he suddenly died I called in old friends on Jack's and my radio show and we told Jack Wallace stories and laughed ourselves silly. Like the time when he and a buddy got tickled at a woman's face in the choir on Sunday morning at a church in Brownwood and had to be led out of the church by deacons as they roared with laughter.

And his encounter with Lyndon Johnson is a sure cure for anything from gout to gall bladder infections. I frequently called Jack during his all-night show and disguised my voice to make him think it was Lyndon Johnson. Jack finally caught on. Then one night the Vice President of the United States really did call Jack to request some information. Whereupon Jack replied, "Well, this is Martha Washington. Come down and get it yourself."

I'm not sure but what Jack's reaction to that blunder wasn't a factor in his rather early demise that cheated me and the audience of the funniest partner I will ever have.

Buck Steiner

Buck Steiner, among other things, was once one of the largest producers of rodeos, a title since inherited by his son Tommy. His Brahma bulls have thrown many a cowboy many a mile. Yet there are a lot of people who, if faced with the decision on whether to be penned with a Brahma bull or Buck Steiner, would need time to consider. As a matter of fact, some folks would tell you that Buck is about half Brahma himself. It would not be out of character for him to paw the earth with his foot and snort in rage when confronted. Buck is known far and wide as one tough hombre, and I suspect justifiably.

Buck runs Capitol Saddlery in Austin. He sells saddles and bridles and boots and ropes and anything he can get a good buy on. Charlie Dunn, the legendary bootmaker, used to make boots for Buck. But Buck will be the first to correct you when you say you bought a pair of Charlie Dunn boots at Capitol Saddlery. He'll tell you as quick as a bull ride that Charlie made Buck Steiner boots.

Buck is pure cowboy and you'd figure a mite redneck. Paradoxically, Buck Steiner became something like a folk hero to the University of Texas hippies that roamed the drag back in the sixties and seventies. You'd think they would have approached him with all the apprehension of a turkey heading toward Thanksgiving. But they loved Buck. You'd see more long hair at Capitol Saddlery than in Berkeley. Now the fact that the flower generation was also the leather generation, and Buck sells leather goods, might have been a factor. However, I suspect that the tough Mr. Steiner related to the independence of the youth of that era and to their less than reverent attitude toward government.

Tommy Steiner came to see me one day. "Cactus, I'm not sure what this is all about but Dad wants to give you a pair of boots. Dad never even gave me lunch money!" he said.

I went to see Buck, always one to look a gift horse in the face. "Buck, I hear you want to give me a pair of boots," I said.

"Go in there and get my new bootmaker from Lucchese's to measure your feet and pick out the pattern you want," he barked.

A month later I came back to pick up my boots. They were and still are the most beautiful boots I've ever seen in my life: cream-colored ostrich skin with a variety of cacti, some in bloom in greens and browns, inlaid with a truly artistic touch.

"Buck," I said, "these are the most beautiful boots I've ever seen! How can I ever thank you?"

"Well, they're not for you," he growled. "Those boots are for your late daddy. Back when I was a kid and didn't have enough money to buy bread your old man used to let me in his cowboy picture show free. And you can tell anyone who asks that these are Skinny Pryor boots, and they are worth five hundred dollars!"

I wear my Skinny Pryor-Buck Steiner boots with more than pride. I also wear them with the knowledge that even Brahma bulls have their soft spots.

Sam Cobb

Sam and Carolyn came roaring up in front of our Port Aransas cottage in their white jeep covered in happy flower decals. With his round belly in full view and his white beard and mustache he looked like Santa Claus. He laughed like Santa too, from the bottom of his toes to the top of his bald head. And when Sam laughed, Carolyn laughed, co-happiness immediately evident.

"My name is Sam Cobb," he roared from the jeep. "Roy Swann over in Corpus says you're looking for someone to go fishing with. Get your gear and let's go."

For several delightful years after that it seemed like I was always getting my gear to go someplace with Sam and Carolyn—be it a mad dash in his boat out to the kingfish waters from Port Aransas or a cross-country drive to compete in a retriever field trial.

Sam and Carolyn lived in an O'Neil-Ford-designed home in Dallas. My friend O'Neil never met my friend Sam. But had he known him, the San Antonio architect would have designed that very same house for him—comfortable, open, happy. When my retriever Ol' Yeller and I would come to Dallas for the north Texas retriever trials, Sam and Carolyn would accompany me. We would train in the pond behind their home and in the field fronting their property.

Then one wonderful Christmas a friend gave Sam a Lab pup. His name was Shadow of Aspen. You wouldn't have found a recognizable name in his pedigree. He was meant to be just a pet. But Sam had caught the field trial fever and set out to make Shadow a field-trialing dog. He did a marvelous job teaching the animal his basic training. But when it was time for the advanced training, Shadow learned that Sam had a problem. A heart condi-

Two winners: Sam Cobb and Shadow of Aspen.

tion restricted his physical activities, and it was apparent to Shadow that he could do just about as he pleased when he was a good distance from his master. Sam knew that he was a walking time bomb, that his heart could go at any minute. So he and Carolyn moved to Austin, and we formed a partnership. I would help Sam with Shadow's college training. Pedigree notwithstanding, Shadow was obviously an outstanding athlete. He soon was placing in competition at an age when most dogs are just beginning to prepare for advanced field trial work.

That dog became Sam's life. They were more than a team; they were best friends. I constantly had to remind Sam that you don't give a dog ice cream cones after it has been disobedient. Sam would spend his day preparing for the late afternoon training sessions for which I would rush from the studio. Carolyn and my young son Dayne became our assistants, and Sam would brief them on the day's training session with the efficiency of the big business executive he had been before his illness.

He gave it all he had. You could see the strain. When he was quiet you knew that pain was his companion. But when Shadow did his work well, the legendary Sam Cobb laughter would come exploding from that great belly out of that happy mouth like a merry volcano. He remained alive to see Shadow compete. Shadow gave Sam the trophies and ribbons that are so difficult to come by. He gave him a reason for going on. And when the field trial season was over, so was Sam's. He checked out of this world still beaming from Shadow's accomplishments, which had given him a couple of bonus years on this earth. Carolyn hired a plane and spread his ashes over the Gulf of Mexico, over the blue waters that so often called us. Blue water and blue ribbons, how he loved them.

Sam was not there the day Shadow and I won the Dallas Open and he became a Field Champion. But Carolyn was, and she said Sam was too. They're together now, Sam and Shadow, where the water is always blue and the ducks and pheasant are plentiful and accommodating.

Bill Kuykendall

We called him Wild Bill Kuykendall because he was wild and his name was Bill Kuykendall. Not wild in the crazy sense—well, maybe sometimes—but wild like a deer or a hawk: A man of nature more at home with sky and land and water than with concrete and steel.

Not that Bill was anti-people. He had to have them; otherwise, who would listen to the stories of one of the great storytellers of his time? When Bill told a story he told it with his whole body: his mouth, his eyes, his feet, his hands. He made campfires a magical theater. He had great recall and had an adventure-filled life to call on for memories. He also had the knack of not allowing the truth to get between him and the telling of a good tale—a necessary quality.

And the stories *about* Bill Kuykendall are legend. There were the polo days when Bill and a team of ragtag Texas cowboys led by the immortal Cecil Smith went east with their cow-trained quarter horses and devastated the fancy dudes of the country club polo set—not only with their polo, but with their "don't give a damn" manners. They still remember in polo circles the day that Bill and another player rode the length of the field fistfighting each other on horseback.

Bill's wife, Alice, still shakes her head incredulously when she recalls the evening she and Bill were leaving their Kyle, Texas, ranch for a black tie social in Austin. As they were pulling away from the ranch house, Bill noticed a big, heavily antlered whitetail in his horse corral. Alice sat mesmerized as her tuxedoed husband cornered the huge buck.

"Surely he's not," she thought. "But yes, he is," she concluded. "He really *is* going to bulldog that deer!"

Perhaps Bill's happiest days were when he operated a 200,000-acre cattle ranch in the Burro Mountains of northern Mexico. He was able to live the life of 100 years ago for which he was meant. The ranch was accessible only by airplane; therefore, Bill, even though in his sixties, went to his friend, Bobby Ragsdale, in Austin and bought a Cessna 180.

"Now show me how to fly this machine," he ordered.

An instructor took him up for an hour or two of dual instruction, whereupon Bill commanded, "Now show me how to fly this thing to Eagle Pass."

There they went and shot a landing or two on the airport runway.

"Now let's head down to my ranch."

They flew the 150 miles over treacherous country and landed on the dirt landing strip that came with Bill's ranch.

"Now let's head back to Eagle Pass."

The patient instructor complied and they landed once more at the border town.

"Well, I sure do thank you for teaching me how to fly," said Bill. "There's a bus leaving for Austin in thirty minutes."

"What are you talking about?" gasped the pilot. "You don't even have a license."

"Don't need one in Mexico," barked Bill. "See ya around."

Bill then proceeded to get the plane off the ground somehow and fly back to his Mexican ranch.

And for several incredible years he survived a flying career that would have made Orville and Wilbur have second thoughts. He'd take off downwind, explaining that the Mexican wind socks blew backwards. Once, while flying from his Mexican ranch to his ranch at Kyle, Bill became enveloped in clouds and vertigo set in. He couldn't read the instruments that tell you when you're flying rightside up. So he simply took his jeep keys from his pocket and hung them from the compass. When they dangled correctly, he knew he was not upside down. He survived.

Bill Kuykendall was a whooping crane. And when he left this earth, the species was no more.

A man of the Texas hill country—Charlie King.

Charlie King

Charlie King is the Edwards Plateau. You find all the character of the Texas hill country embodied in this one man. His face contains the deep canyons. It has the strength of the granite hills and when his eyes twinkle, they have the softness of the hidden valleys that catch the topsoil when the floods roar and give birth to tall trees and rich stands of native grass.

Charlie is as much a part of the hill country as are the cedar and limestone with which he has worked all his life. He represents that vanishing breed of men and women who scratched and dug and chopped out an existence in that stingy land. You could have bought it for a dollar an acre forty years ago. It would support only goats, armadillos, jackrabbits, deer, and Charlie Kings. Now Houston money is buying it for up to two thousand or three thousand dollars an acre: The current price of escape.

Charlie went to school in the hill country. He majored in rock-laying, cedar-cutting, and making-do. Making-do means making wire suffice for an engine part you can't afford or creating a meal out of squirrels and wild roots when there isn't enough money to buy food at the store. Charlie constructed a log cabin for me on my little patch of Texas hill country without using a level or even one helping hand. It stands strong and true, a monument to the ingenuity and strength of a then sixty-five-year-old man. It will always be known as the Charlie King cabin.

He is a master sculptor. He can dig those limestone rocks out of the ground and arrange them in pure works of art. He is the Russell of fireplaces, the Umlauf of rock walls.

He is also a superb inventor. He invented the Chevro-

Ford boat lift. This is a boat hoist he rigged out of old Chevrolet and Ford parts. Charlie invented the chicken wire water pump. I guess that's as good a name as any other because chicken wire is what he used to repair my non-functioning machine.

He always apologizes for the charges for his services as if he should be doing his magic for free. As it is, he asks about one-half of what it would cost you if it were not Charlie King doing the job.

Charlie frowns when he looks westward to his beloved hills from his Manor, Texas, home. He sees the results of those who only take from the hills, who gouge out home-sites with bulldozers, who suffocate the earth with pavement and choke the streams with silt and pollution.

Charlie is too old now to lift the rocks and chop the trees. He and his wife are trying to eke out an existence from Social Security, which is an even tougher source than the Texas hill country has been. And his gnarled hands are folded in his lap as he watches the television, but sees instead the hills of the Edwards Plateau still purple and still undisturbed and still part of Charlie King.

Skinny Pryor

Walk up to a movie theater box office sometime and ask the cashier if she'll let you in the movie free if you get her a glass of water. That'll get you a free saliva test as quick as you can say, "But Mr. Skinny used to."

"Mr. Skinny" was my dad, Skinny Pryor. He owned the Grand Central Theatre (everyone called it "Skinny's") on Austin's Congress Avenue back in the days when even President Hoover could tell you that Tom Mix's horse was named Tony and a "talkie" was a noisy neighbor.

Skinny Pryor was the softest touch in town. Every kid who ever went barefoot and rode stickhorses knew all he had to do to get in Skinny's was stand outside the theater with a forlorn look on his face when Dad was selling tickets.

Soon Mr. Skinny would call you over to the box office and his gravelly voice would say, "Got a nickel (the price of admission), kid?"

"No, Mr. Skinny," was the standard reply.

"Well, take this glass and go down to the drugstore and get me a glass of water."

By the end of the day, the theater would be full of "water boys" and the five-gallon can Dad kept by his chair would be full of water.

On Saturday mornings during those depression days, Skinny's would often feature freckle-faced kids' matinees. Any kid with over five freckles on his face would be admitted free. And if you didn't have freckles, Dad would paint them on with water colors.

He was probably the only theater owner in history who gave lessons on how to slip into a movie house. When he'd catch a boy trying to enter without a ticket, he'd give him a short lecture on honesty and then explain, "When you are

Cactus' dad, "Mr. Skinny" Pryor (with pipe).

slipping in, always walk backwards so if you're noticed, they'll think you're coming out, but changed your mind and went back in."

Dad was Austin's babysitter. Mothers would bring their kids in the mornings and leave them all day, secure in the knowledge that Mr. Skinny watched them like a Las Vegas pit boss. He showed nothing but cowboy movies with the exception of an occasional jungle film. Being an ex-vaudeville song and dance man, he knew the value of ballyhoo and on Saturday nights the best show in town was on the sidewalk outside the theater. Dad would walk back and forth, wearing his traditional all-white or black suit with black bow tie and either a derby hat or a straw blazer, shooting a cap pistol.

"Come on in, folks. Cowboys shootin' 'em up tonight! Sit too close to the screen and you'll get powder-burned!" Dad proclaimed.

Between features when there was a good house he'd often mount the tiny box stage in front of the patched screen (kids liked to shoot lead staples with rubber bands at the bad guys) and give a pitch for coming attractions. Sometimes when he was feeling his oats, he'd add a soft shoe shuffle and a joke to the routine. My first experience on stage, and my first commercial, was when he lifted me onto the stage to announce coming attractions.

Another unique feature of Skinny's theater was Uncle Wallace. Dad's brother was projectionist, using machines that pre-dated Edison. Often they broke down—like every fifteen minutes or so. And always it was just before Buck Jones was attempting to jump the high chasm on his white horse, Silver, or Ken Maynard was being drawn on by the guy in the black hat. The kids in the audience would naturally whistle and scream for the movie to continue. Sure as Tim McCoy's shootin', Uncle Wallace's red bald head would emerge out of the projection booth window and he'd bellow, "Shut your mouths! I'm trying to fix the damn thing as fast as I can!"

We were poor, we thought. Five- and fifteen-cent admissions didn't add up to many dollars. But now some forty or fifty years later, when a lone wrinkled former newsboy or shineboy comes up and wants to shake my hand simply because I am a son of Mr. Skinny's, I realize how rich we really were.

Mary Pryor

No matter where I may go around the nation, I frequently have men walk up to me and say, "We have the same mother." And I smile and say, "Yes, we're lucky, aren't we?"

Mary Pryor had six of her own. But then she adopted, or was adopted by, thousands of other boys.

Mother began her professional career as a cashier at my dad's theater in Austin at the age of sixteen. She retired from show biz a few years later when they were married. That career was to resume many years afterward in 1948 when Dad died. Mother went back to the theater and tried to make it work. But "Skinny" Pryor *was* the theater, and it wouldn't play without him. At the age of fifty, with this stint as a theater cashier as her only work experience and six kids later, Mary Pryor started looking for a job to bring in the money that no life insurance policies provided.

Fortunately, a friend of mine, Aubrey Black, suggested a position for which Mom was eminently qualified—being a mom. The Phi Gamma Delta fraternity at the University of Texas in Austin needed a housemother. She applied for the job, but the head of the selection committee thought she was too old for the position. Thirty years later when she retired, that same man confessed, "I thought Mrs. Pryor was too old to be our housemother, and now she looks younger than me."

The Pryor boys had prepared "Holy Mother Mary," as we call her, for almost anything, including World War II. We were to parents what beans are to chili—unthinkable and practically intolerable. So Ma did just what came naturally; in the process thousands of Phi Gams fell in love with Mary Pryor.

No bridge-playing housemother, this Danish gal. She was in the kitchen helping the cook, or upstairs fussing at the boys for leaving their rooms in such a mess, or in her apartment giving a troubled young man some loving motherly advice. She didn't shirk from the rowdy frat parties. She stayed with them to the red-eyed end, riding herd on an ever threatening wild stampede. And when things started to get out-of-hand, she knew which fraternity leaders to go to for results.

I doubt if any fraternity ate better than those thirty years of Mary Pryor's Phi Gams. Her mother, who spent the first fifteen of her one hundred and one years in Denmark, was a Rembrandt with a wood cookstove. Mother was the beneficiary of grandmother's cooking legacy, as were the members of Phi Gamma Delta. Nothing was a stronger incentive to persuade rushees to pledge Phi Gam than Ma Pryor's meals. Even us Pryor boys and girls would jump at the invitation to come to the frat house for dinner.

When mother started seeing the same names on the pledge lists—sons of members she had known—then she knew it was time to start thinking about retirement. She'd make up her mind to leave, but then the boys would serenade her, or give her yet another locket (they gave her scores) and beg her to stay, and she'd give in.

Finally, in 1980, thirty years after the "too old for the job" housemother began, Ma Pryor stepped down. The Phi Gams gave her a retirement party that was more like an inauguration. The exes came literally from all over the world to fill the Super Drum. They showered her with gifts, including a ticket to Denmark. The president of the University of Texas presented her with a beautiful citation for unexcelled contribution to the University of Texas. The Phi Gams serenaded her, and then scores of grandchildren serenaded her. Mary Pryor stole the show as she wowed the adoring crowd with a loving, humorous, sincere response that left few eyes dry but her own.

Some mother I've got—me and thousands of other guys.

A. D. Stenger

We associate east Texas with the unexpected. Who would have suspected that the arid Southwest could produce a vast fairyland pine forest? Who would have dreamed that well diggers would be thwarted in their search for water by underground lakes of oil? Who would have thought that this bedrock Baptist and Methodist stronghold would give birth to the parents of the sexy Dallas Cowboy cheerleaders, the Apache Belles, and the Kilgore Rangerettes? And who would have believed east Texas' biggest surprise, A. D. Stenger?

I got the notion that a mold had not yet been made for A. D. one Super Bowl of a day on the serene Bay of La Paz in Baja California. Our fishing boat was gliding almost as smoothly as an ice sailer on the calm, blue waters. I had begun to expect the unexpected from the architect-builder Stenger, but when he removed the anchor from its rope and started fashioning a loop, I began thinking saliva test. Frantically he directed the saucer-eyed captain towards a tiny hickie of an island. On top of this dot was a huge sea lion lolling languidly where he and his ancestors had languidly lolled undisturbed by man nor beast for eons. As we neared the creature, Stenger's mission became apparent. He intended to rope that sea lion! Fortunately for all concerned, he missed. But A. D. Stenger was to rope again.

The next episode opens in Spitzenberg in far northern Norway. The small Texan with the big rope procured a sixteen-foot open boat, a fifteen-horsepower Johnson outboard motor, and an unsuspecting Norwegian guide named Tule. Not to worry that A. D. spoke no Norwegian and that Tule spoke no English. There was plenty of toilet tissue on which to communicate by drawing pictures. And this they did for six unbelievable weeks.

A. D. Stenger with his bears.

A Norwegian freighter deposited them a scant 600 miles from the North Pole, and the man said he'd see Stenger and Tule later—if the two were lucky. In the small boat the Texan and the Norwegian ventured further north than man had been before in such an illogical craft. They survived ice storms, hungry polar bear raids on their food supply, and they barely made a rendezvous with a boat bringing them gasoline, without which they would have been hopelessly stranded in the arctic wilderness.

But their most dangerous encounter was yet to come. One day they spotted a polar bear swimming across a bay. Quickly they cranked up their tiny motor and pursued the huge creature. As they neared the bear, Tule sensibly handed A. D. his rifle. A. D., not so sensibly, handed the rifle back and reached for his Texas rope. Around and around he swung the loop. Then he tossed it. The expression on that bear's face was akin to the look on the Norwegian guide's, as he realized for the first time that his client's mission was to rope a polar bear! The bear decided he was not born for rodeos, and the furry creature cut out to sea—ten miles out to sea—hauling the crazy Texan and the fear-crazed Norwegian with him. Finally, deciding that he'd had enough of this madness, the bear turned and started pulling his way to the boat by the rope, paw over paw. Just before becoming bear burger, A. D. grabbed his rifle and accomplished yet another first by becoming probably the first man to bag a polar bear with a .22 caliber gun.

That bear—all nine feet of him—is standing now in A. D. Stenger's Austin den right next to the figure of a Norwegian guide transfixed, frozen from the moment the Texan's rope slid over the neck of that mammoth bear.

Tom Attra, the "battling newsboy."

Tom Attra

The two of them stood toe to toe, hitting each other as hard as they could hit for three torturous rounds. No other two men in the city could have withstood that pounding. Buddy Sommers, light heavyweight champion of the U.S. Marine Corps, won the decision of that Golden Gloves fight. But Tom Attra, with that fight, had begun a boxing career that saw him win two national Golden Gloves titles and a short, successful span as a professional.

Tom was known as the "battling newsboy" because he sold the *American-Statesman* as a kid on the streets of downtown Austin. After his career as a fighter, he was placed in charge of all the downtown newsboys, before they were mainly replaced by cold metal dispensers. The same heart that enabled Tom Attra to stand in the middle of the ring and slug it out with a man intent on knocking him senseless was filled with tenderness for the less fortunate. Those newsboys, many of them handicapped, were Tom's children. Never was a mother hen more caring for her brood. Their problems were his problems. What a champion to have in your corner!

Tom was known more for his on-the-street antics, however, than for his troop leading. He's about as inhibited as something Red Adair would charge one hundred thousand dollars to extinguish. Tom likes to bark. Some people find that strange, especially when the bark has just been delivered into their ears from the rear. I'm not a bad barker myself and many the time Tom and I have engaged in a barking bout with one another across Congress Avenue. It won't get you a goose up the corporate ladder, but it's not a bad way to greet a friend who shares your joy of life and the art of barking.

After more than fifty years with the publication, Tom left the *Austin American-Statesman*. It was rumored falsely that a remark he made in the newspaper office might have forced his exit. Someone said, "Tom, are you as punchy as people say?"

"No," replied Tom, "if I were that punchy I'd be editor of this outfit."

One of Austin's old hotels took Tom on as a doorman. It didn't work. They didn't have the proper appreciation for a doorman who not only could carry more luggage under one huge muscled arm than three bellmen could handle but who also barked at anyone who got in his way.

There have been many miracles in Tom's life. All his adult life he was known for his raspy, croaky voice. As he grew older it became almost a whisper. Then one day a doctor found a tumor in Tom's throat, removed it, benign—thank God—and now Tom's voice is as clear as the bell that begins and ends each round.

Tom Attra is being inducted into the Austin Sports Hall of Fame. Good choice for this man of many victories. And perhaps his last fight as a pro was his greatest one. He was offered a sizable amount of money to throw the fight. Tom responded by going to his father, who was dying, and saying, "Dad, this fight is for you." He knocked the man out in the third round. His father died a few days later knowing that his son was still a winner. Tom Attra remains one.

Walter Yates

It was during World War II on one of those shell-shattered islands of the Pacific. A young United States Marine from Texas was crawling on his stomach through a Japanese-dug tunnel. As he inched around a turn, he came face to face with a Japanese soldier. For an eternity that lasted but a split second, they stared at one another. They both moved for their weapons. The Marine moved faster and won his life.

The young Texan was Walter Yates, now 55 years of age. At last report Walter is missing somewhere in Canada. He went down in his helicopter for some unknown reason while trying to return to Austin from his beloved Alaska.

Walter has been carrying on a flirtation with danger for many years. Perhaps that encounter with the Japanese soldier during World War II gave him a feeling of destiny to live. There's not much Walter has not done. He has built and flown his own helicopter. He has parachuted out of planes. He has spent a winter in complete isolation in the arctic wilderness of Alaska in a cabin that he had built himself, using primitive tools. He has climbed mountains. He has flown planes over places where there was no possible place to land, including Siberia.

Once, on a flight to his cabin on the Post River in Alaska, he had a serious engine problem along with bad weather. Only a miracle could save him from disaster. The miracle occurred. His overheated engine cooled with a drastic change of weather and he survived. During his lonely winter in Alaska another miracle was required when he was caught in a blizzard many miles from his cabin. He made his own miracle and made it safely back to shelter.

Walter Yates at gold-prospecting site in Alaska.

Walter introduced me to flying. I have flown with him thousands of miles. We have been in some tight spots together. But I was never really concerned, because I have great faith in his ability as a pilot and as a survivor. Once, over Anchorage, we almost had a head-on with a private plane off its course. Another time, taking off from a beach on the Texas coast, we had run out of beach and time when a gust of wind lifted our plane into the air at the last possible second. An errant weather forecast once caused us to fly through a tornado-laden front that was destroying scores of airplanes on the ground below us.

On all of these occasions Walter was unshaken, calm, and in command, as if he knew there was a special guardian looking over him. I feel that that special guardian is within Walter Yates, that it dictates his decisions, his actions, and whatever the force, it's enhanced with Walter's horse sense and hours and hours of doing his homework in the matter of survival.

At this recording, Walter Yates is still down in Canada, but I'm giving odds that he's not yet out of this world he so dearly loves, that he has at least one more miracle within him.

EDITOR'S NOTE: Walter Yates, badly injured but alive, was rescued a few days after Cactus delivered this commentary. He is now back in Alaska, mining gold and flying helicopters.

Eulogy to My Mother-in-law

Well, Lord, we're sending you a good one. One of the best, a real pioneer woman. They don't make 'em like this anymore, Lord. So we know you're going to enjoy the company of Ora Lee Allison Holiday.

But you *know* her. You've been watching her for ninety-two years now, and you've been proud of every minute she was on this planet. She served you well in her own special way. I don't know who could have done a better job of looking after nine children almost single-handedly.

You graced her, Lord, with the tenaciousness and the courage to persevere in that raw west Texas land where dust storms and tornadoes and rattlesnakes and hunger ran off weaker people. She not only took the adversities in her stride, she made them bow to her will. She beat the dust storms with wet rags and a strong broom. And she used the same to beat the meanness out of some rear-ends that needed a good strong broom. A lot of headless rattlesnakes attested to her prowess with a sharp hoe. She was awful good at beating hunger too, Lord. She had a special recipe for biscuits: Three cups of flour, teaspoon of baking powder, tablespoon of lard, pinch of salt, and a large dab of love. With some cornmeal and pinto beans, she served a meal that made those enjoying it glad there was a depression so families had to exist on such simple fare.

And she was a sharer, Lord. She never turned a hungry person away from her door, be they a neighbor's kid or a hobo riding the rails trying to find a way out of the depression. You've written much about this kind of kindness in your book, Lord.

You filled this woman with love, Lord, and she gave of it unsparingly. She gave of it by chopping wood with the strength of a man, and by turning right around and giving all the tender, loving softness that the sufferer of a stubbed toe or a skinned knee needed to make it well.

And Lord, you blessed her with perhaps the greatest gift of all—a delicious, hardy sense of humor. She was a joy to be around. She made us laugh with her juicy choice of words and phrases, even unto the end. I suppose she laughed a lot in defiance—daring adversity to overcome her with gloom. She chuckled the most, like any good mother hen, when surrounded by her own brood. She loved her children with a love that only you can appreciate, Lord. She loved to tease them and be teased by them. She got more out of family love than most people get out of all their fancy manmade pursuits put together. And that love was returned to her by every single child, full measure, and they should feel good about that.

She cared about people, Lord. Even in her last days she seemed more concerned about her fellow patients than herself. Yessir, she was an embodiment of the spirit that made this frontier habitable.

Ora Lee was the very essence of the characteristics of the early Texas woman, a pioneer in every sense of the word. Without the likes of her, there would not have been the likes of us to enjoy the pleasures of the trail they blazed.

We thank you, Lord, for giving us this noble lady for so many years, so many extra years. Her leaving is made less painful by those bonus years and the knowledge that she has a special place with you. Because Ora Lee was—no, Ora Lee IS a very special woman.

Shaking hands with a fellow Texan, President Lyndon Baines Johnson.

A Tribute to LBJ

One of our neighbors died yesterday.* He died where he most enjoyed living—at his ranch just a short distance from the waters of the Pedernales, so important to one who works the land along its banks and who draws peace of mind from the ripples and reflections and sounds of water in a dry land.

He died within scenting distance of the barbecues he enjoyed giving for friends underneath the huge oak trees alongside his house, within calling distance of the cattle he enjoyed summoning for food, within hearing distance of the bells of the little church across the river that he often attended, and he died within walking distance of the rodeo grounds across the way where he often enjoyed the rancher's sport of men against livestock. He died near his beloved deer and dove and horses, and on a crisp, clear day that so often lured them together.

Our neighbor was the thirty-sixth President of the United States, Lyndon Baines Johnson. Death came to President Johnson in the same way the presidency had come and ended—suddenly, unexpectedly.

Thousands of us in this part of the nation are fortunate to have known this man as a neighbor and friend. He was quite a neighbor. He was a magnification of the western tradition of a man helping his neighbors by barn raisings, quilting bees, cattle roundups. In earlier years this spirit of neighborliness had sometimes meant banding together with your neighbors to withstand the attack of marauding Indians or fighting prairie fires or a frantic ride in a bouncing buckboard to deliver an ill or injured friend to

*January 22, 1973

155

the doctor in the town miles away. It often meant pushing a lathered horse almost past its endurance to summon the midwife for a neighboring expectant mother. And when the crop-damaging storms came, bringing hail and flood or sleet and snow or clouds of dry dust, it was the western tradition to help your neighbor feed his family as he would help feed yours.

His contributions to those of his beloved hill country will forever be remembered. The same attitudes and resulting contributions transcended the limestone and cedar country. His neighbors included camel drivers in Pakistan, cowboys in Mexico, and children in Thailand. As President, he associated with the great leaders of the world. But as a man, he was always motivated by the frontiersman's genuine concern for the welfare of his neighbors.

The world now knows that we have lost another president. The years will prove that we have lost more; we lost a neighbor when Lyndon Baines Johnson died yesterday.

J. Frank Dobie

The old man and I were friends before we knew each other. He was "old" simply because I was so young. I would often walk from our home on Speedway Street to Eastwood Park where Waller Creek had dug out my favorite fishing hole in the limestone rockbottom. I was always armed with a cane pole, earthworms dug from our backyard worm bed, a brown bag full of mother's "world's best fried pies," and the conviction of a young boy that the fish would be big and hungry.

Eastwood Park was a place of magic. The tall stand of trees provided haven not only for the squirrels and birds but also for Daniel Boone, Robin Hood, and, on certain magical days, Geronimo. I caught more dreams than fish in that special fishing hole by the cedar bridge—stringers full of them.

I sometimes shared this catch with the old man. I'd look up and find him standing there on the bridge, leaning on the handrail on his elbows, smoking that curved pipe and watching me. When I'd wave, he'd speak. "I didn't want to get in the way of your thoughts," he'd sometimes say. "A feller catches some real important thoughts when he's fishing."

Sometimes he'd come down and accept my offer to enjoy some of Ma's fried pies. Other times he'd just lean there on the bridge and watch. We didn't talk that much except about fishing and fried pies and squirrels. We didn't even know each other's names. We never asked. We just accepted each other as fishin' hole friends. He'd stay until his pipe ran down. Then I knew that he'd soon be heading up to his pretty, two-story white house a short distance away for a refill.

Age got in the way of that fishing hole, as I exchanged it for others. It was years later when I again encountered my old friend. I was invited to the ranch of J. Frank Dobie, an opportunity to sit at the feet of the gods, the Texas triumvirate of Dobie, Walter Prescott Webb, and Roy Bedichek. When these three unique, earthy intellectuals got together with nature and Jack Daniel, those who were within earshot were blessed for life. As I was introduced to my host I learned, for the first time, the name of my old fishing hole friend. Mr. Dobie didn't recognize me. The kid with the cane pole had grown up. But he was kind enough to remember when I recalled the days.

There were a few other visits to the Dobie Ranch during these delicious twilight years of the three magnificent conversationalists. I learned more about the world and about the dignity of the individual in those warm bluebonnet afternoons and cedarfire evenings than in all my days of schooling. It was a crash course in bird watching; Shakespeare; vocabulary; city, state, national, and international politics; bean cooking; horse breaking; and corporation damning. The conversation ebbed and flowed like fine blue smoke from a well seasoned pipe. This was what learning is supposed to be like.

I conducted the last interview J. Frank Dobie ever granted a member of the media. I told him that he had made that little fellow with the cane pole the luckiest fisherman in the world.

Bill Moyers

He looked like a typical young kid who had just come to the big city from East Texas—as he had. His glasses seemed too big for his face and his words seemed too big for his age. His intelligence shone through like a July Texas sun. He had the Texas Baptist look; the glasses were part of it, the joyous smile, the outstretched hand and hurry-up gait. And the name was right for a Texas Baptist—Bill. Bill Moyers.

He had come to Austin to attend the University of Texas and to work at KTBC television and radio in Paul Bolton's news department. Word was that he had been handpicked by LBJ for his wife's station. LBJ had a knack for picking exceptionally bright, energetic, ambitious young men for employment. He had been such a young man himself. So Bill Moyers with his Marshall, Texas, newspaper experience and his Baptist preacher training entered the world of radio and television.

He couldn't have trained under a better person. Paul Bolton was a veteran newspaperman who had covered the Texas Capitol beat with the likes of Walter Cronkite and Van Kennedy. He was chosen for the job of news director because he *was* a newsman, the age of cosmetic news reporters not yet having afflicted the television industry. So young Bill Moyers got a basic education in basic journalism, the advantages of which are so apparent in his present reporting.

The news department consisted of four people, including editor Bolton. They reported both radio and television news. But the energy of young Moyers in essence gave KTBC a much larger staff. With his pad and pen and sophisticated television camera equipment (a Polaroid camera), he rivaled cedar pollen for covering central Texas. At the same time he was taking a full schedule at the University of Texas and preaching Sunday services as a lay Baptist minister. His sleep consisted mostly of fifteen-minute cat naps.

He still found time to unleash his fiendish sense of humor, which ran to practical jokes. I was beginning a fifteen-minute radio newscast one day when the sound of a loud explosion startled my audience and me. The explosion had come from beneath my chair where Moyers had thrown a very large firecracker. There was another explosion shortly thereafter as I caught Bill one block away at 7th and Brazos, having left my radio audience in unexplained silence.

Upon graduation Bill left us for bigger things. I next saw him in Houston in Lyndon Johnson's hotel suite. Bill was Senator Johnson's constant companion during his and John Kennedy's campaign for the presidency. Moyers had not slept for weeks. I was an advance man for the Houston appearance of LBJ. We had inherited him the evening of that dismal day in Dallas when he had been spat on. The Senator's mood was just a dab brighter than that of a water buffalo wounded and deprived of water. I had not done a thorough job of making hotel arrangements. As a matter of fact, I had done a lousy job of making hotel arrangements. LBJ chose to have me join Moyers and Marvin Watson in his suite. There for three straight horribly long hours I received for the first time the legendary LBJ lecture and the unshakable conviction that politics was a career to avoid like hydrophobia. As I glanced at Moyers for support I received instead a Cheshire cat grin. Still remembering that lecture at 7th and Brazos, eh, Bill?

The Magic Valley

Is the Rio Grande Valley of Texas really as magical as they promote? Around two or three o'clock in the afternoon in the middle of July when the wind is as calm as the humidity is high, the magic is hard to come by. But at sunset that same day, when the sun is hunkering down behind the horizon, silhouetting the rows and rows of tall palm trees and giving promise of kinder temperatures, and when an evening of margaritas and delicious steak and quail waits across the border, the magic works.

When the evening television weatherman delivers reports of twelve below temperatures in Minneapolis and a blue norther raping Amarillo and you must decide between golf in McAllen or surfing at Padre Island on the morrow, then indeed, the Valley is magical.

The Rio Grande Valley is full of serendipities. I remembered driving from Los Angeles to San Diego in 1945 and being surrounded by orange trees all the way. I retraced that journey in 1980 and was shocked to see that the orchards had vanished. But I rediscovered them. They had been moved to the Rio Grande Valley.

We drove across a little tinker toy bridge over the Rio Grande to a dusty little Mexican town called Nuevo Progreso where the progress was so new it was not evident except in a wonderful cafe called Arturo's. The tequila sours were intoxicating in flavor alone. The steaks were tender and juicy and more than filled the huge platters they were served on. The frog legs and quail would have made a traitor of the strictest vegetarian. And I still salivate twenty years later at the thought of those hard little football-shaped rolls, *bollos*, served hot and filled with melting butter. Magic indeed.

Perhaps the most special aspect of Valley life is tempo.

If a New York minute is thirty seconds, then a Brownsville minute is ninety seconds. Even the non-Spanish-speaking people understand "siesta." It's interesting to watch the "snowbirds" who come flocking in with the northern winds from Canada and the Midwest succumb to the Valley beat and unwind and let go.

There's even a certain magic in watching that ant-like flow of people back and forth over the port of entry bridges stretching over the chocolate Rio Grande. As I see that ebb and flow of humanity that continues almost unabated between the two countries I'm always reminded of the incredible sight of the waters of the Pacific and the Gulf of California merging in contrasting colors at the tip of Baja California like runny oils on a canvas.

There's black magic in the Valley. The easily accessible vices offered up by the have-nots for the haves do strange things to people. The cause of international relations is furthered every evening in the "Boy's Town" bordellos of Matamoros and Reynosa. And the sight of cowboys, both urban and real, dancing with the *senoritas* in the saloons that front the bedrooms magically erases 100 years of time.

Yes, the Rio Grande Valley is abracadabra land. And the best trick will be if it can avoid turning itself into another Florida east coast as the magic of the valley is discovered by the masses.

Confessions of a Border Rat

I am a border rat. Put me between Mexico and Texas in the canyons of the Big Bend in a rubber raft going down the Rio Grande, and I'm in heaven. And in an isolated little cantina in some lost and lonely Mexican border town, if the beer is cold and the music *puro ranchero*, I'm not exactly in agony. Put my feet under a table at the U.S. Bar and Cafe in Reynosa or at the Cadillac Bar in Nuevo Laredo, and I'll stay awhile and be in a good mood.

It's not the tequila; as a drinker I wouldn't even be worthy of Carry Nation's attention. Besides, the tequila sours and margaritas at most of the border bars are to drinking what Mexican food is to eating—it's better on this side. No, it's the atmosphere. The sounds, the sights, and the smells.

I was in Brownsville recently at the retirees' golf mecca that is Rancho Viejo. The cocktail party preceding the banquet I was attending ran late, so it was nine o'clock before we were served dinner. The shrimp in the shrimp cocktail had been netted just that day a few miles south of our dining room. The steaks were tender and lopped over the side of the platter on which they were served. Although I had had no lunch and was starved, I did not touch my food. I was saving my hunger for something very special.

As soon as I finished my speech at 10:30, I ran for my rented car and made a famished dash for the Drive-In Restaurant in Matamoros. This is one of my favorite eating places in the world. I don't know why they call it the Drive-In. It is not a drive-in. And the name certainly does not reflect the menu, which could rival the finest in Paris— France, that is, not Texas.

There were quail and venison, frogs' legs and chateaubriand, red snapper or redfish caught that day, and cherries jubilee and baked alaska—all to ponder. I went for the basic T-bone steak, however, which is accompanied by fried onion rings, thick fried potatoes, and salad at the Drive-In. But more than all, I feasted on the *bollos*, the hard little dinner rolls that can be duplicated in appearance, but never in taste, on this side of the border. They have to be made in Mexico to be that soul-satisfying. And the Drive-In serves the very best *bollos*, hot and crispy and ready to be filled with butter.

With the dinner came the serenaders with their strings and guitars to sweeten the margarita that needed a little sweetening. The waiters remain the same throughout the years, as familiar as the menu. They're efficient, courteous, and wisely only semi-literate in English so as to give you an excuse to use your high school Spanish. But they're fluent in the showbiz preparation of the flambeau dishes. You flinch a little when the waiter brings you *la cuenta*. Still, it's low enough to bring you back.

And of course, like any good border rat, I stop at the liquor store to buy the traditional kahlúa. And then a sleepy drive back to the motel, grateful that calories garnered in Mexico don't count in Texas.

Only in Houston

Houston is probably the most dynamic city in America, if not the world. She is a giant sponge soaking in people with an insatiable appetite—would that she could soak up the humidity as well. It is ironical that the city that energy has built and is building has the least regard for conservation of the stuff than perhaps any city in this nation. People stop and stare if they see more than one person in an automobile. You get the feeling that if Houstonians could drive two cars at once they would; and frequently they do—your car and theirs.

If you are young and ambitious and daring, this is the city for you. Opportunity and burglars will knock your door down to get in. I had my Houston opportunity—one year of it. Ambition, however, should be made of sterner stuff. My tempo was three-four. Houston is four-four and upbeat. It's hard to waltz in a traffic jam.

I was reminded of my decision to leave Houston and why I made it on a recent trip there. I was driving at 11 a.m. in the morning from Main to the Galleria on Westheimer. Westheimer Avenue is Houston in a capsule: on the right a chili parlor next to a body painting shop—no automobiles accepted, only drivers. A funeral home next to a saloon next to a secondhand car dealership. The arrangement makes more sense if you're driving in the other direction. Now a stately old Victorian home stands in quiet indignation at being a neighbor to a dirty book store. Flashing signs: Totally nude girls; tacos and beer; carburetors tuned and brakes realigned for a steal. And then an improbable oasis—a church school. Holy white buildings stand surrounded by soft green grass, neatly trimmed shrubbery, freshly scrubbed children. Even the morning smog seemed to swerve around the property in reverent respect. Now the shell of a once proud building standing grotesquely like a huge piece of toast burnt beyond salvage.

And then, in a typical Houston context, the entrance to proud, pompous River Oaks—from Baghdad to the Riviera in instantaneous non-zoning. Now a pawn shop almost lost in the shadow of a modern highrise building. Looming through the byproducts of refineries and automobile exhausts like faint ghosts wading through swirling fog stand the outlines of the famous Galleria and the accompanying buildings.

And you realize that you've been driving bumper to bumper in 11 a.m. traffic. Wait until the rush hour. Houston, you beautiful big baby giant! You make no sense—only dollars. No other city is better equipped to heal the wounds of its citizens nor to inflict them. The world's first indoor football field housing a team owned by the likes of Bud Adams. Polyester and milk. Gilley's and Brennan's. Brown and Root and Marvin Zindler. She is as unzoned in people as she is buildings. As my car finally broke free from traffic on Interstate 10 heading west, I looked back at the skyline I deserted, and she never looked better.

Life on a Houston Freeway

It was like a scene from Apocalypse. A gray cloud enveloped the morning, part fog, part carbon monoxide, part Mount St. Helens, perhaps. There was a steady roar that penetrated the windows of my automobile even above the sound of the radio. It was the noise of the daily mass held in Houston, Texas.

I'm talking about the movable mass oozing from their suburban homes down Interstate 10 all the way from Katy to their downtown offices. Even at 6:30 a.m. the line was uninterrupted. The tide coming in. Though I was going against the automotive train, the three-lane expressway of which I was a part was extremely busy, even at that early hour. The pavement is no longer just concrete and asphalt. By now it is rubber, oil, gas, bones, matter, dried blood, ground glass. The expressway has that ugly color that you find in the large cities where the streets never escape the onslaught of traffic.

The guardrail and fence that separate the southward traffic from the northbound traffic on Houston Interstate 10 is like a dog-eared page on a well-read book. Every 100 yards or so an interruption—stark evidence of a sudden stop that resulted in tragedy. The bent steel and torn wire reminding the rushing but unheeding throng of the always present danger of collision. I noticed the inward traffic had slowed and the ominous reflection of the red and white rotating beacon cut through the morning smog. Soon another dog-eared page unfolded. Two huge dinosaurs lay wounded across their trail. A couple of large trucks had collided, the front of one grotesquely disfigured, the windshield devoid of glass, the other monster lying on its huge caved-in side, a large gash exposing its cargo of paneling. Another souvenir for the fence. It was all a little insane.

As I put myself further from the accident the inbound traffic remained backed-up for miles. You could see the expressions of frustration on the uneasy riders' faces as they endured the delay. Now it was official. The traffic reporter on KTRH had reported the accident and suggested that those traveling in that direction avoid the unavoidable delay.

As I finally left the city limits of Houston and rested my eyes on the gulf plains country stretching from Katy to Columbus, I contemplated my joy at not being a daily witness of that mad scene. That many cars, mostly carrying just one person into a city that, more than any other, should be aware of the energy crisis, makes no sense.

And yet even the mayor will tell you there's little being done toward mass transit in Houston. I gloated in my Austin smugness all the way to our city limits, where my gloat rapidly disappeared. The crunch of traffic threatened to make me late for my television show.

Sheppard Field, Texas

What do you do in Wichita Falls, Texas, when you've got some spare time? Well, if you were in the United States Air Corps during World War II undergoing training at Sheppard Field there were a lot of things to do—like catch dust pneumonia or play hate-the-drill-sergeant or go AWOL to some nice place like Death Valley. After six weeks of basic training all of us trainees had concluded we had met the enemy and they were training us.

We called our base Colonel Clagget's Concentration Camp. Colonel Clagget was the commanding officer. Rumor had it that he had been stationed at Pearl Harbor when the Japanese attacked. We figured he had been the officer in charge of the early warning system and had been exiled to Sheppard as punishment. Better that he had been on the Bataan Death March.

Life was not all grim at Sheppard Air Force Base, however. There were compensations like four solid hours of sleep each night, all the potatoes you could peel, and free lessons in profanity from the captain—and he was the chaplain.

Then there was the train near Jacksboro. Let me explain. The only thing drier than the drill field at Sheppard were the bars in Wichita Falls. Liquor was not sold, at least legally, in the city. Oh you could buy 3.2 beer at the base PX. It was a blend of Kool-aid and sheep dip—if you drank a case you couldn't even work up a headache. But the train! At the confluence of Archer and Jack counties near Jacksboro there was the greatest beer joint in Texas. It was an open field planted knee-deep in khaki-clad airmen. Jack County realized there was a war going on and wanted to do something for the boys in the service and their country.

So on certain days a train would pull up, unhitch a boxcar loaded with beer, and blow the prettiest whistle a thirsty man ever heard. By evening time the prairie field was the Trianon Ballroom, the Palladium, the Coconut Grove, and the Waldorf Astoria all in one big mass of humanity. The Nazis could have dropped a bomb on that alcohol-saturated plot of earth and done more damage than was done at Hiroshima. Not that anyone would have cared. Care was lost by that railroad track outside of Jacksboro. Gone were the thoughts of forced marches, barracks inspections, k.p., army chow, and "Dear John" letters. Entertainment came in dark brown bottles, and even Sheppard Field seemed palatable in this yeast-smelling oasis. Miracles happened. Soldiers smiled. There was singing. Why, I even once saw a sergeant with his arm around a common airman.

I often wondered what happened to that field after the war. A memorial should be erected there with a citation reading: "We the men of the United States Air Corps, World War II, dedicate this plot of earth to immortality for its unceasing efforts in easing the pain of the damnable plot of earth called Sheppard Field." I hope it's planted in daisies or roses or some other sweet-smelling, soft plants— and, if beer fertilizes, they should be growing in profusion.

Barton Springs, U.S.A.

People used to set their watches by it. It must be three o'clock because here come Skinny Pryor and his kids for their daily dip in Barton's. Nothing came between Dad and his daily swim. He had been known to take a nip before his dip and many the time I've seen him dive into that sobering cold water, swim his daily two-and-a-half miles, then roll over on his back in the middle of the pool and go into a deep, sound sleep. He had natural buoyancy that he passed on to every member of our family but me. And many a bather has been startled by the sight and sounds of a man lying on his back in the middle of the swimming pool, snoring like a freight train. Then, when it was time for Dad to go back to work, we kids would swim out to him, take hold of his big toes, and literally tow him (no pun intended) back to the bank.

We were force-fed Barton Springs. One doesn't naturally take to those frigid waters. I can remember hating those daily baptisms. I would sit on the bank hoping Dad would forget the swimming lesson. But always it would come. He would lift me up and dunk a shivering mass of goose pimples into the icy water, carry me a few feet from the bank, give me a little shove, and I would struggle and choke my way to safety. Then a few more feet away, and then a few more. And then, by your third birthday, if you were a Pryor, you were expected to swim all the way across that spring-fed ocean. Unfortunately, my birthday comes in January, but I made it and somewhere between Dad and the shoreline I learned to love Barton Springs.

Mothers didn't have much time for swimming in those days. Momma would join us, though, on weekends and holidays. Dad was a freestyler; he had a slow, slow stroke that concluded with a loving pat of the water he so adored. Momma was a side stroker. Women just naturally swam and rode sideways in earlier days. I suppose facing forward has been part of their liberation. We were always delighted to have Momma join us because that meant picnic lunches on the grassy shores under the big pecan trees. Cold fried chicken, watermelon made cold by a dunking in the nearby springs, sometimes a freezer of homemade ice cream. And all our young lives we were reminded to wait at least thirty minutes after eating before going back to swimming—an eternity. And now the experts say that it is not true that swimming right after eating will give you cramps! A lifetime wasted waiting on the banks.

Often in the evenings we would stay for the sing-songs led by Dan Greider. We'd spread our blankets on the grassy slopes, competing with people and chiggers for space, and sing away the troubles we didn't have anyway.

Barton's took on a new meaning when I got to courtin' age. High school dances were held on the wall-less second floor of the big wooden bathhouse. Glenn Miller and gardenia corsages and a smooth cheek against yours, because touching was allowed during these ancient dancing rituals. Then at intermission a hand-in-hand stroll along the banks of the transparent water, watching the catfish and bass swimming around looking for a handout. And I'm told that other extracurricular activities took place on the darker, grassy hillsides.

One of the pleasures of parenthood has been introducing my children to the luxury of Barton Springs. Now I wonder, will my children's children be so blessed? It appears doubtful.

Port Aransas

"I must go down to the sea again, to the lonely sea and the sky," wrote poet John Masefield. Yes, it is an indisputable truth. Once you have tasted "the gull's way and the whale's way" you must come that way again.

But why? Had Masefield ventured forth in a craft such as mine, would he have felt the same about the sea? His vessel was a tall ship with white sails shaking and with a star to steer her by. My unwise choice is a sixteen-foot Glastron with a Johnson outboard motor, a craft designed for pulling water-skiers in calm inland waters, and not for carrying the chicken of the sea out of sight of land.

But each year I'm drawn almost mystically past the safety of the jetties leading into Port Aransas to the blue waters, usually miles out into the Gulf of Mexico. Each year I feel the same inner tremblings as I experience those rough seas that always seem to be guarding the entrance to the channel, daring you to come out into the world of water. I know my concern is justified, and the pale silence of my companions, my children, tells me they concur.

I am the type of weekend sailor who must be an anathema to the Coast Guard. No real knowledge of seamanship. Only a small compass and the firm conviction that if it points to the east going out it should point to the west coming in. No marine radio to use should I need to call for help. It is an unwise journey. But I ease my trepidations somewhat by setting visual goals. First the marker buoy a half mile or so out from the end of the jetties. Then the whistling buoy a few miles further. And then the comforting sight of something occupied by man out in those foreboding waters, an off-shore drilling rig. I head for that and circle it a few times, hoping to find the king mackerel that are my excuse for venturing out into these deep waters. But they are not there, so I reluctantly leave this possible haven and seek another, a shrimper anchored several miles further out to sea. I head for it, glancing anxiously shoreward to make sure Port Aransas is still there.

As I move toward the shrimper, I discover it is not anchored, but is moving toward the horizon. Hitching up my courage, I move further out to sea. When Port Aransas sinks behind the waves and only water is our companion, the fight-or-flight instinct becomes a tug of war. Fight the fear and hang on or to hell with it and turn the boat with my most precious possessions aboard to fly homeward?

Then the kingfish usually come to our rescue. A silver ribbon fish attached to one of our lines lures the magnificent battlers that make you forget all else but the thrill of the encounter. It is his fight and his flight that now occupies you. By then the morning calm has set in and the ominous waves have flattened to skiing boat size. The morning gray of sea and sky have turned to magical blue and the kids have found their voices. And you even find the courage to turn off your motor and just float with the swells.

The serenity of the sea envelops you, just as strongly as the danger of the sea had consumed you. And you remember why you are really there. Not for the fish, but to be at one with the sea, the lonely sea and the sky.

The Rape

Well, we've done it. We've soiled our nest. We've contaminated our sacred waters. To many of us the water of Barton Springs is sacred. Many of us were baptized into the true church of God when we plunged into that icy cold, pristine body of spring water. And now that pool is contaminated with bacteria. This is an insult to the memories of Barton Springs addicts like J. Frank Dobie, Roy Bedichek, Bob Morrison, and my dad, Skinny Pryor.

I heard it thunder the other night and I thought, "That's Mr. Dobie reacting to the news that Barton Springs has been closed due to a high bacteria count in the water." It would be fun if he were here. He would unleash the anger that made him sit out a traffic citation in jail rather than pay the fine that he thought was unjustified.

I can hear him now: "Barton Springs contaminated? It's like blaspheming your own mother. It's like stabbing yourself in your own heart. These waters that have been gushing forth from the limestone rocks of the Edwards aquifer for eons are the lifeblood of this community. This is what our life here is all about. We have chosen a place to live where we can live in harmony with nature, not in opposition to it. Just as the Indians had the good sense to make their campgrounds around those springs of pure water, we've had the good sense to make our homes in this Texas oasis. Barton Springs is much more than a swimming pool, it is an attitude, it's a statement for quality of life. There's been more philosophy taught sitting in the sun next to those magical waters than in the entire forty acres that make up the University of Texas. There have been more sound political decisions made at the feet of those majestic ancient pecan trees guarding the pool than in all the smoke-filled rooms of the houses of state. There's been more poetry inspired and romances begun at Barton Springs than anyplace I know. It is our rebuttal to those who say: 'One must devote one's life to the pursuit of the almighty dollar no matter where the venture may take you, no matter what the personal sacrifices, no matter what the cost.'

"This pool of water is sanity and now it is suffering from the insanity of man. Barton Springs is a microcosm of the world in which we now live, with its disregard for traditions, for the natural, for the precious. This is what we have come to—fecal bacteria infecting our very life-blood. It's the end of the world that we have known. Damn, damn, damn."

I don't think I'm presumptuous in speaking for the late Mr. Dobie. I only hope I'm not speaking about the late Barton Springs. We'll see.

Save Us, Willie Nelson

Willie Nelson, come rescue us, quick! Austin is in trouble and the outlaws are about to be consumed by the non-outlaws. For a precious while, Willie, you personified Austin. You brought your outlaw brand of country music that dared to be different from the Nashville product. You dared to shun the spangled shirts and sculptured hairdos. Country music branded you an outlaw, and Austin loved it because this community has always danced to a different beat. Willie, you were right for Austin, and Austin was right for you.

But Willie, the corporations are heading us off at the pass. We're still dancing but the beat is being dictated more and more by the non-outlaw corporate guys in New York City, Detroit, Los Angeles, Dallas, and Houston. They're buying us out, Willie. They've bought all the television stations. Most of the radio stations. They own the newspaper, the department stores. A locally owned bank is rarer than a loan without collateral. Same way with the savings and loans institutions. Gone are the days, Willie, when you could get a loan simply because the banker knew you or your family.

They're choking us with sameness. Same food, same suits, same music, same newscasts, same everything, Willie. They're trying to standardize us. It's easier for the corporate non-outlaws if we fit the mold they have made. It's better business for them if we conform; of course, business is the name of the game, not individuality.

Homegrown is not a corporate word, Willie. Oh, they start out friendly enough. They say that they're buying people, not a business. But those words are just as dangerous as a Texas politician saying, "I'm just a dumb little ol' country boy." Invariably they gradually start doing things their way, the proven way. They feel compelled to bring in those who have fit their mold elsewhere. Their machine calls for interchangeable parts. They want to be sure that their dancing partners will follow their beat.

It's not the growth that has got us in trouble, Willie. We can take as many as we can hold and still be a very special city. It's the attitude that's the problem, the attitude that says if it's good—strike "good," that's not the factor—make it read, if it "worked" in Boston, it'll work in Austin. And the danger is, it *will* work in Austin, Willie. They'll pour enough money and effort into it to *make* it work. And that means they'll get what they're after—money.

But another result, Willie, is that it'll take the outlaw out of Austin. We'll be dancing just to their beat and soon you'll be able to dance to the same tune all over the nation and never miss a step.

Come home, Willie. And strike a blow for freedom. We're not losing our hills, our lakes, our swimming holes. We're losing ourselves. The outlaws are becoming interchangeable corporate robots force-fed a franchised diet. Save us, Willie Nelson, save us.

Born Again Texans

Texas is now homogenized. The Sunbelt has had to let out a notch or two to make room for all the new citizens moving into our area of the nation. Dave Braden, my funny architect-speaker friend in Dallas, says we're guarding the wrong border.

Native sons in Houston are harder to find than parking spaces. You hear more Yankee whine than Texas twang in Dallas nowadays. Used to be you had to go to a zoo to see a Republican in Texas. Now we've got one in the governor's chair. Vendors are having to learn that "pop" is something you drink besides someone you hit up for lunch money, and "you guys" can be used instead of "y'all." Next they'll be serving hamburgers in Texas without lettuce, tomatoes, and onions. You really can't blame the newcomers for coming here. How you gonna keep 'em down on the farm after they've seen the homes on the range?

I know a few snippy Texans who don't want our new citizens. I remind them that if Davy Crockett and Jim Bowie and a few of those transplants hadn't had the travel itch we might be shouting "Hook 'em Horns" in a bullring while sipping tequila sours.

It's going to be interesting to watch who changes whom. Will Texas change the newcomers, or will they change us? It is an interesting social question for our culture which is, in many ways, completely foreign to those who have moved here—say from the New England states. I mean, have you ever heard of chicken fried lobster or a Boston bean cook-off? And, conversely, many of their proclivities are strange to us—like exercising restraint at Dallas Cowboy fumbles and remaining seated when the band plays "I've Been Working on the Railroad."

I was discussing this question with a Texan the other

day. I said, "I wonder if Texas will change the new Texans or if they'll change us?"

He stretched out his long arms attached to his six foot five inch frame, kicked the dust with his weathered boots, tilted the time-beaten Stetson back on his sunburned face, expertly spit a squirt of Redman on the back of a fly, and drawled, "Well, little bittie buddie, I look at it this way. When you're lost and wanna git home you give your hoss his head and he'll git you there. I figure there's just a bunch of them Yankee folks that have been lost and looking for a home a long time. Now they done gave their hoss a loose bridle and he's brought 'em to the home corral.

"You can take a Texan out of Texas but you can never take the Texas out of him. But you can *brang* a non-Texan to Texas and you'll never get him out of Texas, if he's got any brain at all in his head bone. No sir, us Texans don't change, and ain't no Yankee gonna make thangs any different a'tall around here. No difference a'tall."

The man was an IBM employee who had moved here from his hometown of Hartford, Connecticut, eight months ago.

Never Take a Rooster to New York

If you are ever invited to take a rooster and thirty pounds of frozen venison to New York City on an airplane, don't do it. I speak with great authority, for on one occasion I consented to do just that.

John Henry Faulk was living in an apartment in downtown Manhattan. That alone should have made me suspicious—always question the wisdom of one who chooses such a lifestyle. But John Henry did have the good instincts to miss certain aspects of the life in south Austin that he had forsaken. He especially missed being awakened in the morning by the crowing of a rooster. So he prevailed upon his friend Helga Krial, daughter of Carl Sandburg, to give him a male chicken. It was a magnificent creature that combined the best of two worlds, being one-half jungle fowl and one-half English Frizly. For reasons that best go unstated John Henry named the rooster Joe Small after his western magazine publishing friend of the same name. The problem was that the fowl was delivered to Faulk's Austin address, and John Henry and his wife Elizabeth were living in New York. That's where I bungled into the picture.

"Since you're coming up here to stay with us for a few days, Cactus, would you mind bringing along Joe Small?"

"Why no, I'd love to. Joe is one of my best friends."

I only later learned that *this* Joe Small was covered in feathers and dug chickens that weren't fried.

"Oh, one other thing, Cactus. My nephew, Guich Koock, has given me some frozen venison. Would you mind bringing that along too?"

Stupidly, I didn't mind.

It began well. I checked Joe Small in a small cage with

my baggage. The thirty pounds of venison were wrapped in aluminum foil and frozen hard. So I put it in a paper sack and carried it aboard with me. All went well until we were over Washington, D.C., where you expect something to go wrong. The pilot came on the intercom and explained that due to a blizzard in New York our jet would be unable to land at J. F. Kennedy. However, they would land at Dulles and bus us to Washington National, where we could catch a propeller job that would fly us to La Guardia.

We landed, frantically grabbed our luggage, including Joe Small, and climbed aboard the bus for National. By the time we arrived there, I noted with alarm that the frozen venison was getting soft. And as I left the bus and ran for the terminal a steady stream of blood was flowing from an apparently badly wounded brown paper sack. Knowing that I wouldn't have time to check my luggage, I covered Joe Small with my topcoat and boarded the plane with the rooster under one arm and my bleeding sack under the other. Just as I got to my seat, Joe Small decided it was morning and began to crow as only a combination jungle fowl and English Frizly can.

"Sir," said the hostess, "your topcoat just crowed."

"I know," I replied. "It's made of the finest rooster skin."

Only the plane lurching forward kept Joe and me on board.

Joe Small became a legend in Manhattan. Psychiatrists had a bonanza treating patients who claimed they were hearing roosters crowing in downtown New York. The creature became a great conversation piece at John's cocktail parties as he wandered among the guests searching for worms. And I have dedicated the remainder of my life to avoiding flying roosters.

Art Smart

Art is in in Texas. Starving artists are eating well. Art festivals are doing booming business all over the state. Texans who heretofore would think of Linkletter when you mentioned art are paying thousands of dollars for paintings. So, if you're not with art, you're not with it.

I think I enjoy art as much as the next guy. Certain artists can put certain paints on a piece of canvas and turn me on. But I can't tell you why. Apparently that's important in art—being able to explain why you are turned on or off by a painting. A feller ought to be able to like or dislike a piece of art just like eating okra. If you like it, eat it; if you don't, don't, with no explanation necessary. However, I can verbalize my lack of appreciation of okra better than I can my dislike of certain art; eating okra is like eating greased lizards.

Anyway, feeling left out I went to an art exhibition the other day. I was determined to be with it. I invented my own vocabulary of art appreciation, and it sold like Picasso (who I had just learned was not a cello player).

My companion was a gushy amateur art collector, and I let him have shots like: "Ahhhhhh, now there is a stroke. Notice the delicate subtleties almost disguised by the obvious flamboyant. Don't you think so?"

My friend thought so.

Then I hit him with: "Oh! Shades of Leconosee. If I didn't know better I would say this was Leconosee in a modern idiom. The shading, the touch, the boldness. This has got to be proof that reincarnation does exist. Am I imagining it, or is this Leconosee reborn?"

My artistic friend 'lowed as how it sure did remind him of Leconosee, too. Leconosee, incidentally, plays short stop for a 7-11 semi-pro team.

We went to another painting, a field of bluebonnets with oak trees, and I reacted with, "Haaaaa. Look at this. Isn't this delightful? Haaaaa. Who would have chosen this approach for such delicious satire? Look at the disguised comedy. Now there is an artist with a juicy sense of humor, wouldn't you agree?"

My friend managed a couple of weak laughs and confessed that he sure found it amusing too.

We came next to a painting of a nude female. Now if there's one subject that art connoisseurs and rank amateurs can appreciate jointly it's a nude female.

But I lay this one on my arty friend, "Oh, too bad here. It's obvious what he was trying to say, but it doesn't come off."

My friend stammered, "Doesn't come off?"

"Well, obviously the clothes came off but his message doesn't. You see a naked woman, right? But what else do you see? Nothing, right? The painting is obviously obscured by the nudity. In other words, the body talks but not the painting. Can't you see it?"

My friend studied the painting for five minutes and then admitted that he could see it too.

We came to a Rembrandt and I really did my friend in. "Well, even the masters can have a bad day."

"Uh, bad day?"

"Yeh, obviously this is one that was done during Rembrandt's depressed period. See the grays, the browns. You've read of Rembrandt's depressed period, of course."

"Of course."

"This was done during that time, obviously."

"Obviously," my friend concurred.

Incidentally, now my friend never buys a piece of art without calling on me first for my approval.

Southern Notables

I received a letter recently, informing me that I had been chosen as one of the "South's Notables." As such, I was to be honored by having a one-paragraph biography of my life published in a book that would include other such notables. Immediately I was suspicious. I didn't want to have my name printed alongside a bunch of other people who were comparable to me. Not even misery wants that kind of company.

I became more suspicious when the letter asked me if I knew any other southern notables worthy of being included in such a publication. If they're notable, how come these people have to be notified of their notability? And all of my reservations were confirmed by the last paragraph of the letter. For only twenty-five dollars I could purchase a beautifully leather-bound volume of this book listing all us notable folks.

I wrote them the following letter:

"Gentlemen:

Thank you for the honor that you have bestowed upon me and for having the foresight to recognize the qualities in me that no one else has had the good judgment to perceive. I accept your designation of being a southern notable with great humility.

I have included the one-paragraph biography of my accomplishments that you requested. I'm sorry that it's such a long paragraph, but three single-spaced pages were the best I could do. If you must delete any of it, you might cut the part about the chicken pox, mumps, and dislike for liver and okra. If this still doesn't meet your space requirements, you might prune down the hilarious part about the time I was caught skinny-dipping in the University fountain, but everyone I tell that story to really gets a kick out of it.

As to other notables I might recommend for your book, I have enclosed a five-page list. I'm especially anxious that you contact names number five and number seventy-eight. Number five is the math teacher who failed me in algebra four straight times. I'm sure this lady is notable among all those who studied under her. Number seventy-eight is the former owner of the most heavily attended pit bulldog fight arena and rooster fighting ring that the state of Texas ever boasted. You can write to him in care of the Ellis Unit, Huntsville, Texas. You might notice that I have suggested the names of dozens of other residents of this same address. All of them are notable for one reason or another.

I have included in my list the entire roster of the Texas Legislature. They are all aware of their notability and take great pride in it. Therefore, I feel sure that you will find them anxious to be included in your publication. I have included the names of Billie Sol Estes and Ben Jack Cage. However, this is probably redundant since I am sure you already have them listed in your publication.

You will find the list of twenty-five very popular young ladies who certainly should be included in a listing of southern notables. However, they may be a bit difficult to locate since the Chicken Ranch has long been closed now.

Incidentally, I have decided not to accept your generous offer to purchase a leather-bound volume for only twenty-five dollars. I appreciate it deeply. However, when the world becomes aware of my notability, as it undoubtedly will after your book is published, I'm sure I will be deluged with numerous copies of it from adoring fans.

Humbly yours,
Cactus Pryor, Southern Notable."

I never heard another word from them.

186

Up Your High Cost of Living

My friends John Henry and Elizabeth Faulk, along with their son Yohan and their dog Tabitha, pulled up roots in Austin a few years back and moved to Madisonville. They wanted to simplify their lives and cut down on their cost of living. They learned, however, the problem exists in Madisonville, too.

Suddenly, everyone is wondering why the high cost of living. Naturally, the economists have their pet theories as to why. That is the function of economists: not to solve, but to theorize on why an unpleasant economic situation exists. They'll give you such pet economic clichés as "balance of payments," "depressed market," "gross national product," and similar financial goobledygook. Since anyone who can count to ten with his shoes on qualifies as an economist, I would like to present my theory as to why everything costs more nowadays—and the answer is addition. There's simply been too much addition.

Addition of what, you rightfully ask. Well, like the addition over the years of coloring to margarine, of air conditioning to automobiles, of stick-proof sprays to the bottoms of frying pans without which cooks can no longer cook. There's the addition of electric toothbrushes to our bathrooms, where we have also added colored toilet tissue and mouthwash to which has been added a pleasant taste. Not to mention scores of cans of spray for our hair, our anatomy, our shoes, and the room itself.

To our living rooms we've added color to television sets, stereo to our record players, shag carpeting that we clean with the vacuum cleaner we've added to our cleaning equipment. In our kitchens we've added dishwashers to which we add detergents, water softeners, germ-killers, and Lord knows what all else. We've added ovens that turn themselves on and off and clean themselves, machines to chop and cut and grind and blend and make ice and compress garbage and freeze food and pop up toast. We've added plastic bags for edible leftovers and plastic bags for inedible leftovers, and wraps that cling to sandwiches or seal out odors or in which you can cook the foods. We've added more things that you can add to foods to bring out their natural flavor than there are natural foods to add them to. We've added canned drinks, diet drinks, fattening drinks, and hundreds of new excuses not to drink water. And even to our water we've added softeners, fluoride, and gosh knows how many other chemicals.

To our air we've added coolness and heat that come without command just like the monthly bill. To our bodies we've added colors and hair removers and support and sparkling new teeth and hearing devices and invisible glasses—even improved bustlines. We've added machines to vibrate, gyrate, manipulate our bodies into hopefully different shapes.

We've added enough instants to fill an eternity from soup to bank loans. We've added direct dialing and indirect lighting, selectomatics and automatics, sealers and healers, cheaters and meters, things to dip or zip or rip. We've added a lot of new sets, like the jet set, the skiing set, the golfing set, the antique set.

We've added and added and added but hardly ever a subtraction. And suddenly everyone is wondering why the cost of living has gone up so. Friends, it all adds up.

Coping

Cope. It's a word we hear a lot of nowadays. You never heard it ten or fifteen years ago—not in Texas. But there's hardly a conversation carried on now in which the word "cope" is not used. It's one of those psychologist's specials like "stress," "tolerance," "dry dunk," "vibrations," or "vibes."

It's "in" to "cope" with a situation. Women now are involved in *coping* with being a woman. If you have problems with your spouse you try to *cope* with the problems. If the boss is giving you a hard time, you try to *cope* with the situation.

Perhaps the word has come into play recently because of modern technology. For example, when my mother was raising six kids at home and had to do the washing with an old roller-type washing machine, hang the wash on the clothes line by hand, and hand iron them, somehow *coping* with the wash just wouldn't seem adequate. Just doin' what had to be done would seem more on the beam.

When all six of us were on a rampage and the house was a steaming oven in the middle of a July heatwave without air conditioning, and we were fighting among each other like a pack of hyenas, *cope* didn't actually fit Ma's reaction to our shenanigans. *Backhand* would actually be more appropriate, because that's what she gave us—a backhand across the chops.

Someone asked me the other day, a member of a younger generation, how we *coped* with the depression. Well, actually we didn't *cope* with the depression. We put up with it. You don't *cope* with pinto beans, you eat them when you can't afford meat. You don't *cope* with cardboard in the bottom of your shoes—you just put it there to cover the bottom of the sole and pray that it won't rain. You don't *cope* with the lack of funds to buy enough gasoline to drive the car to town, you hitchhike. And if no one gives you a ride, you don't *cope* with the disappointment, you just walk and hope the cardboard in the shoe will hold out.

We didn't *cope* with the lack of money to buy new clothes, we just patched up what we had that was patchable, and we passed what had been outgrown down the line to the next kid.

Actually, I guess we were too busy *puttin' up with* and *makin' do* to *cope*. Or maybe we just weren't intelligent enough to *cope*.

Coffee, Tea, or Airsickness Bag?

Most of the commercial flights I've been on lately have been delayed at least thirty minutes in their takeoff due to the shortage of air controllers. Anytime I get frustrated by the wait I just shift my mind to recollect and ease into instant serenity. I merely recall the days when I was flying every other week to the Rio Grande Valley aboard Texas International's DC-3, the airplane that has been to aviation what the pickup truck has been to "Fight Gun Control" bumper stickers.

Texas International wasn't Texas International in those days. They were Trans Texas Airways, that's "Trans" as in "across." And that's what I was when I got off one of those dudes: A cross guy.

The company I worked for was operating a radio and television station in Weslaco. My flight would take me to McAllen with intermediate stops in San Antonio and Laredo. I had one basic rule in flying that milk run. Never board the plane without food because you never knew when you were going to get off.

The San Antonio stop on the way down always meant that we would load up with a fresh cargo of "wetbacks." They would be illegal aliens now, but then they were *puro* "wetbacks." The Border Patrol would put them aboard to be met by their counterparts in Laredo, who would escort them back across the border so that they could come across once again. Most of them had never flown in an airplane before. It was a rude baptism, flying in a non-pressurized plane at a relatively low altitude in the bumpy summer air of south Texas. You know the results. And it would take a clean-up crew thirty minutes to mop up the results once we landed at Laredo. Coffee, tea, or Alka-Seltzer?

We continuing passengers were not allowed to leave the plane. There was no portable air conditioning to cool us off, and Laredo in the summer can use all the cooling off it can get. I got enough hot to last me through the remaining winters of my life.

These old propeller-driven planes weren't as reliable as the modern jets. Mechanical problems were the fore-runners to today's television line trouble. You never asked if your flight was going to be on time, but rather, "How late will it be?"

There were compensations, though. You didn't have to worry about your plane being hijacked. No one was that masochistic. Also, I received more education flying to and from the Rio Grande Valley in those ancient carriers than I did in all my formal schooling. I always took books. On one particularly tough flight I began and completed *The Rise and Fall of the Roman Empire*.

You also got to know your neighbor. The twin seats were close enough to give Siamese twins claustrophobia. I always looked for a skinny person with a fresh-scrubbed look to be my flying companion.

Pretty primitive transportation compared to this modern age. But not so bad for one who can remember driving to Galveston from Austin in a Model-T Ford.

You were expecting maybe an ox cart?

The Defeated Air Force

They sat there like a flock of crippled birds blown out of the sky by some unseen force. As our plane landed on the runway usually so busy, I glanced out the window and there, parked all over the taxi ramp, was Braniff's defeated air force, their engines capped and silent, their cabins empty and lonely. I felt as if I were passing a cemetery— as well I was. The jetways leading to the long terminal through which we all have so often frantically run for our departing flights were reaching out and touching the still planes like the umbilical cord connecting a mother to her lifeless child.

I was reminded of the Gregory Peck movie "On the Beach," a story of Australia awaiting the aftermath of a nuclear holocaust that had destroyed the rest of the world. Now the lethal radioactive cloud is drifting irrevocably towards the land down under. Peck, an American submarine captain, sails out of Sydney and proceeds to San Francisco. There they up periscope and view a scene of utter desolation—not unlike the Braniff terminal that I viewed the other day.

It's hard to imagine life without the colored birds. So many memories; so many flights. I recalled the old days when we boarded the airline in Austin from the little tin building that was situated where Ragsdale West's modern terminal now stands. There usually wasn't room to sit, so we'd stand and wait for the old propeller-driven convairs to come rolling up. I contrasted these early flights to a recent trip to Hawaii in Braniff's big orange bird, the 747, sitting in living room comfort, dining on freshly cooked prime rib, and then watching a movie of "The Incredible Flying Machine" as we winged our way over the Pacific.

No longer those happy reunions with fellow fliers in the hospitable Braniff Club at the Dallas/Fort Worth Airport. The smiling hostess greeting you and flattering you by remembering your name—just like she did with most of the other members. No longer the sight of those gorgeous Braniff hostesses (were all of them blonde or did I just imagine that?) hurrying down those long corridors to board yet another plane.

"Where was it today? Are we in L.A. or New York?"

And sometimes slowed by fatigue, dragging their wheeled flight bags like anchors.

"A hard night's flight, eh, honey?"

I remembered the old Love Field days before the airport belonged to Southwest and Muse Air. Braniff meant more than an airline. It meant that they would take me home tonight to my own bed instead of a rented one. And no worry if the banquet meal was slowly served and the speeches as well. Love Field was but a taxi dash away and good old Braniff would get me home.

As I gazed at the Braniff graveyard from my American Airlines window, I recalled the "Pickle Special," Congressman Jake Pickle's lobbied-for flight that flew non-stop between the Texas capital to the nation's capital and non-stop back again. It was profitable during the LBJ years. Texans were in D.C. and Braniff was taking them there. You were sure to see a lot of familiar faces when you boarded that flight. (Often Pickle himself working the crowd like an extra flight attendant, usually a former Texas governor, a newly appointed Texan federal government agency head, a new Texan ambassador. And always the Texas lobbyists winging their way to mecca on the Potomac.) It was a flying Texas party. And then, after the LBJ reign, Braniff brought the Texans home, deadheading it to Washington, but filled to the gills coming back.

As my journey ended the other day, we taxied to the funny little passenger buses that take you from your plane to the terminal in Washington's Dulles. I noted one lone green Braniff bird perched alone and lonely on the concrete apron. That's the "Pickle Special," I thought. Leave her there as a monument to the Texas airline that lifted us up and away and delivered us to the world for so many happy years.